MW01641607

Softcover ISBN 978-1-7364057-0-3
Hardcover ISBN 978-1-7364057-1-0
Digital ISBN 978-1-7364057-4-1

www.touher.com

Printed in the United States of America

For my wife and children who have always believed in me.
Also to the fans and supporters on Kickstarter, without you this book wouldn't be here.

DIASPORA

INK DRAWINGS INSPIRED BY HMONG FOLKLORE AND HISTORY

Diaspora is an ancient Greek word meaning "to scatter about." This is the story of the Hmong diaspora and the culture and history that they try to keep hold of while in foreign lands. Although they have been pushed around most of China and South East Asia, you can now find them in France, Germany, Australia, French Guiana, and the United States. As the new generation assimilates into these countries, the Hmong culture has slowly been pushed to the side and has begun to wither away.

In an effort to preserve some of these stories I've heard and experienced, I created these artworks to help fuel the imagination. I thank you for being a part of this journey and sharing in the collective history of the Hmong people. Whether you are new to experience these stories or already familiar with the history, please share them with others so that they won't disappear with time.

Thank you for helping to bring this project to life. Without your support, this book would still be a dream that I couldn't grasp. This book is for the future generations, may they never forget our past.

Tou Her

FOLKLORE

Hmong folklore is a tradition told by the family elders to the younger generation. They are stories of creation, heroes, monsters, and beliefs told to them from the previous generation. Lessons for the youth to learn and impart to their children one day. A never-ending cycle that holds the memories of a people without a written language. Each clan has its own stories that might differ from another clan. So, listen to the words of the elders as they weave a magical tale for you to carry on to your children.

Folktale

A long time ago, the first man, Lou Tou, lived with his wife. Back when the world was new, the sky was very close to the earth, and it was always dark because there were no lights in the sky. They lived like this for many years until Lou Tou and his wife had a son named Teng Chu.

Teng Chu was an adventurous boy and was always planning for the future. He saw that the earth was too small for their family to grow larger, so one day he asked his Dad, "Txiv, the earth does not seem to have enough room for us. Can you make it bigger, so there is room for me when I have my own family?"

Hearing the reasonable request made Lou Tou see that the earth was too small for them. So, he grabbed the horizon and stretched it as far as his arms could reach. Then he took the sky and pushed it farther and farther away from the earth. Lou Tou had expanded the heavens and the earth so that there would be more room for every- one.

While his father was working on the expansion, Teng Chu spent his time creating two lamps, a golden one for day and a silver one for night. He brought the lamps to his father, and they climbed a large mountain and hung them in the night sky.

Today we can still see Teng Chu's creation above us and explore the large expanse of the earth Lou Tou made possible.

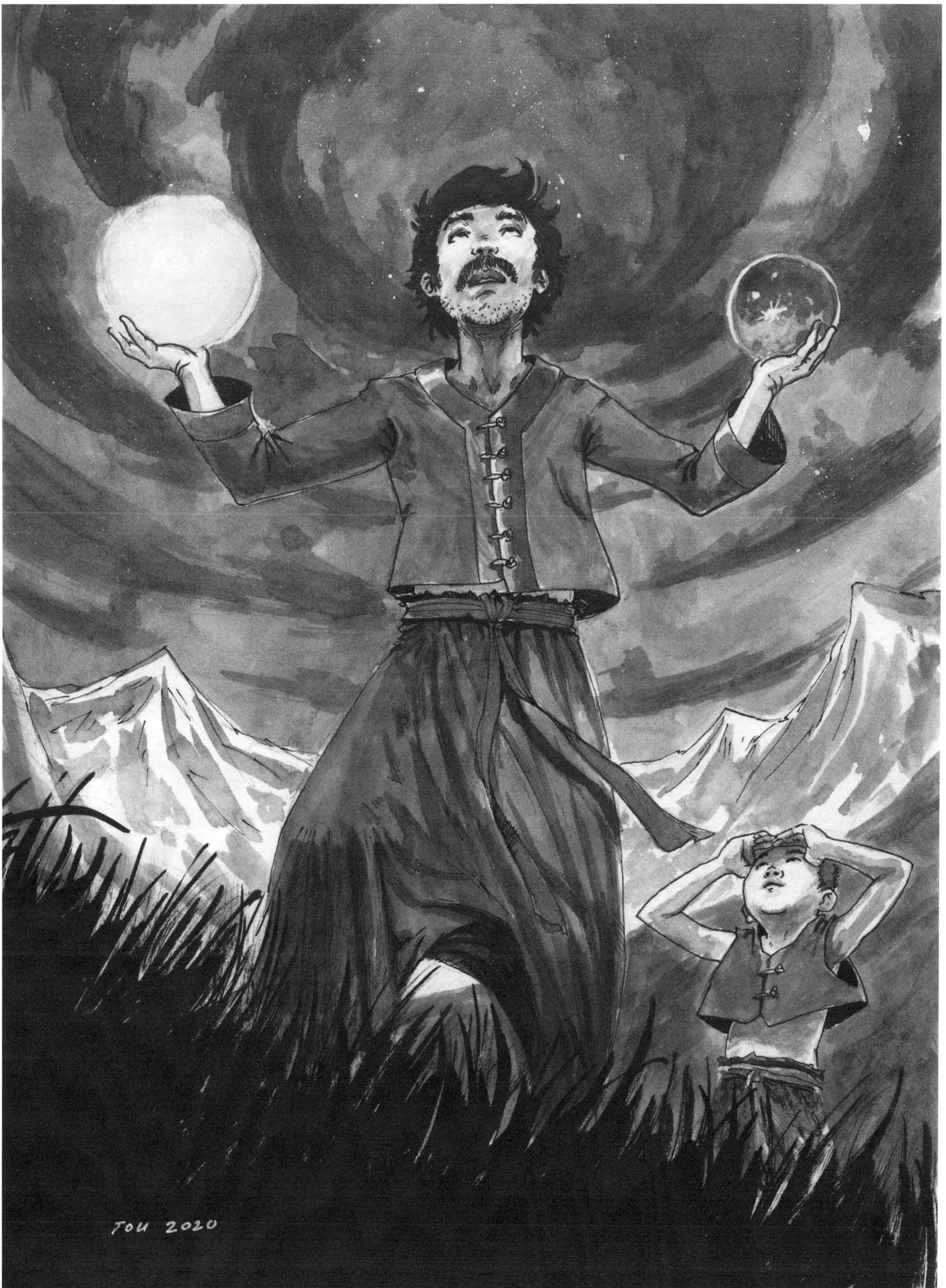
TOU 2020

Drum

A long time ago, the sky opened up, and rain fell in a torrent. For days on end, the water began to flood the land. In a panic, Nruas Nas and Nkauj Mim's parents put them in a big drum and filled it with food and water. As the flood reached their mountain village, it carried them away. For many days they drifted in the waters listening to the rain patter endlessly on the leather drum skin covering them. They ate the food that their mother had put in there for them, saddened by all they had lost.

One day they awoke to the sound of silence. Nruas Nas opened up the leather cover and stared at the large expanse of blue above and below them. There was no sign of land around them as they drifted along. He spotted some driftwood and was able to bring it inside the drum, where he whittled it to hold the leather flap open. As soon as he did so, the drum cover caught the wind, and they sped across the water.

After several days, Nkauj Mim's sharp eyes caught sight of land. She saw three points above the water and directed Nruas Nas to steer them towards it. The mountain peaks were once the tallest mountains on earth, and now only rose a bit above the water. There was enough land for them to start farming again with the remaining plants they had. Upon these mountain tops, they made a home and restarted the human race.

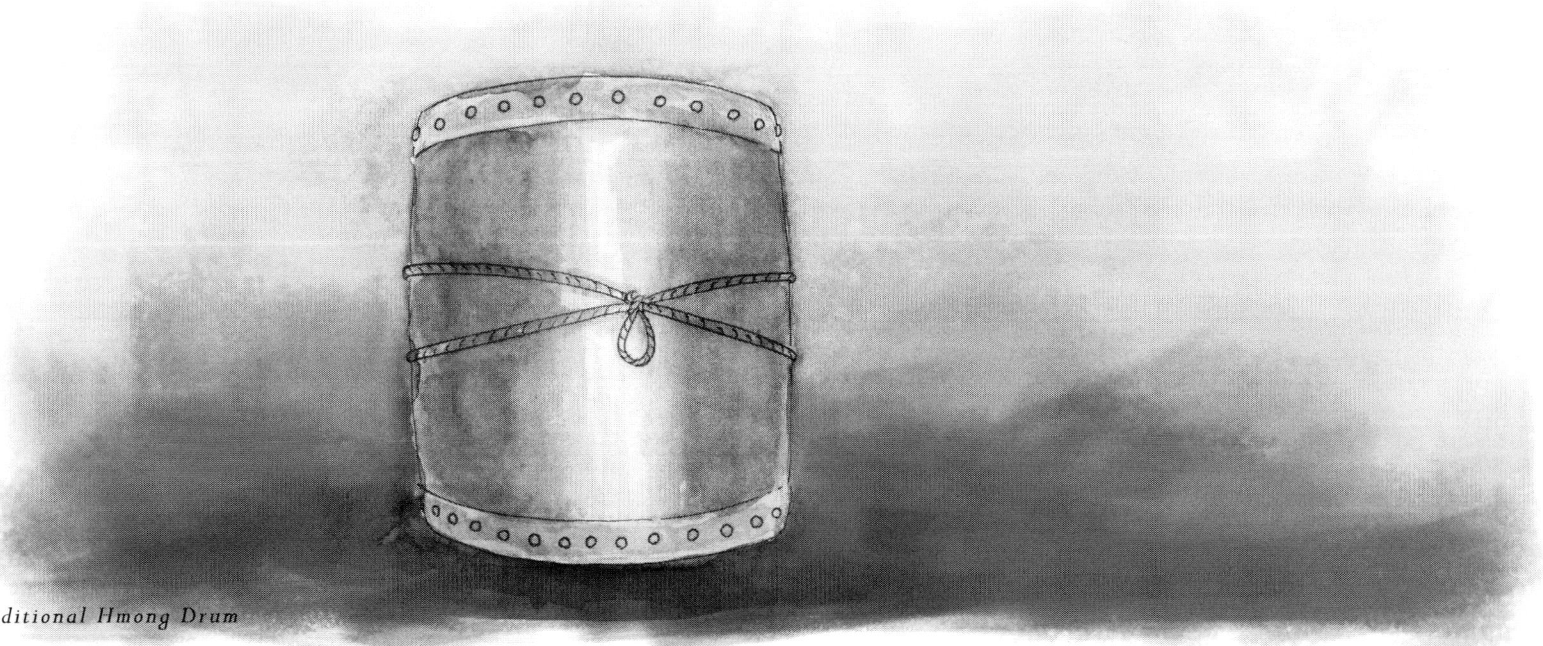

Traditional Hmong Drum

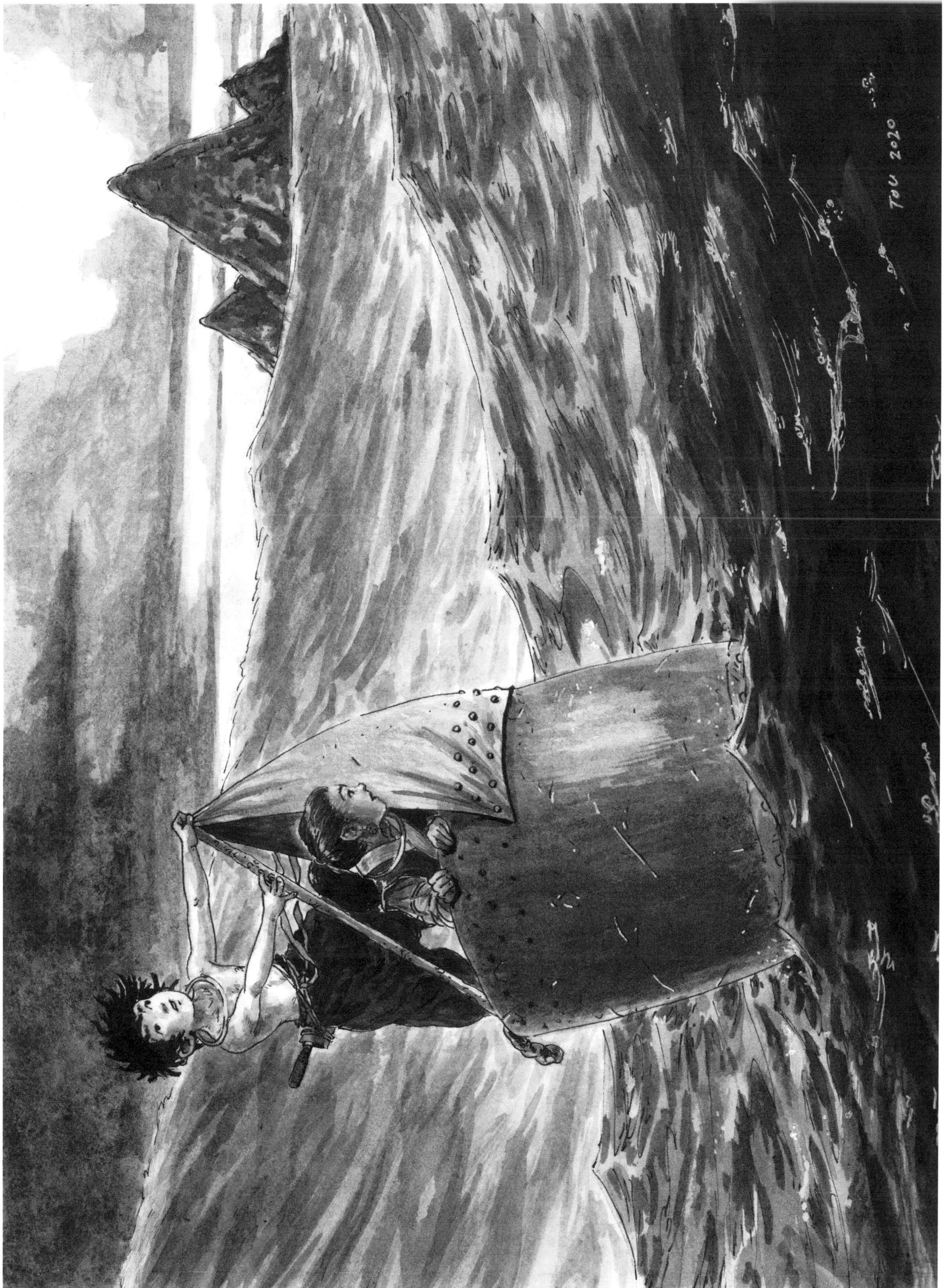

Nam Nkauj Hnub (thelady of the sun) was created to level the mountains and create farmland so that the Hmong can grow food. She was great at her job until one day; she saw her counterpart, Txiv Nraug Hli (Man of the Moon). He captivated her with his look, and she too caught his attention. They spent every moment together and forgot to do their duties.

The Hmong were not happy because they couldn't grow food and complained to heaven. In order to appease the people, heaven let the Hmong people decide the outcome of the two lovers. The Hmong people made their decision and heaven separated the two lovers, Nkauj Hnub could only stay during the day, and Nraug Hli could only appear at night.

Their fate was to be apart and could only sneak an embrace once or twice a year. Today, we call their embrace an eclipse.

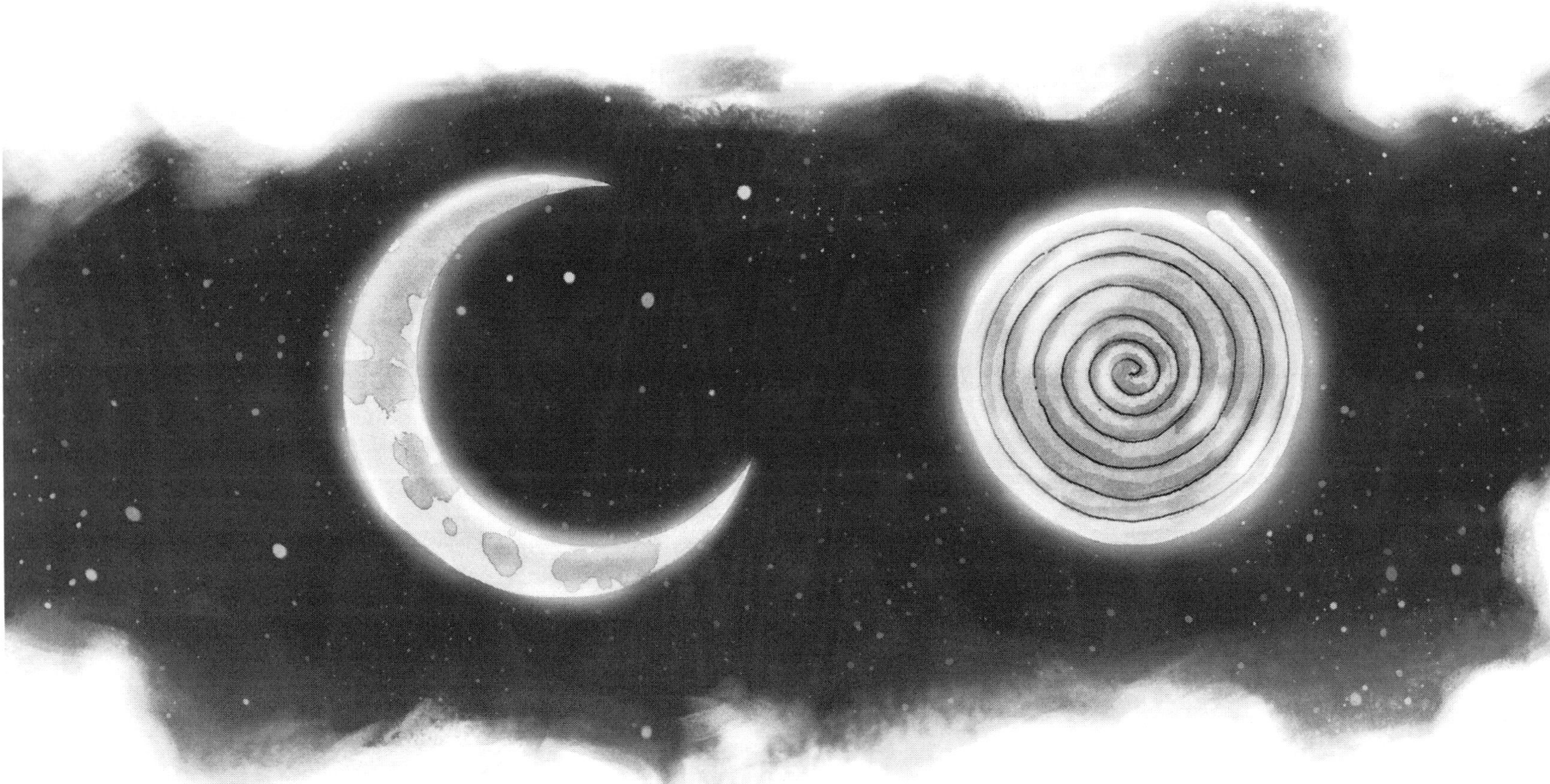

The Sun and Moon torn apart by the heavens

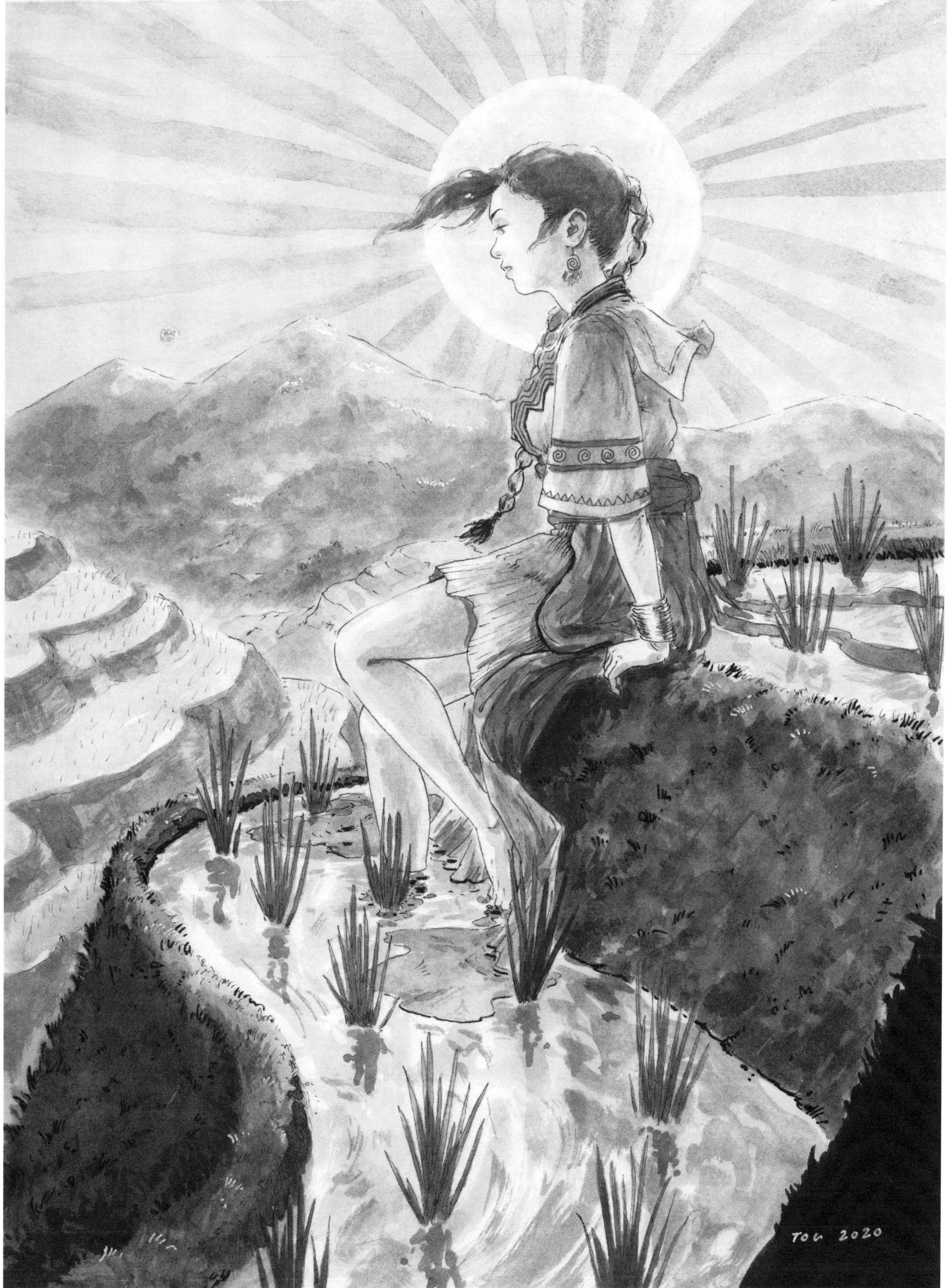
Tou 2020

Nraug Hli sits atop the world after a long and laborious night of work. It had been a long time since he last embraced his love, Nam Nkauj Hnub. He can still smell the sunshine of her hair and the press of her warm skin upon his arms. Alas, each time they were together, the Hmong would make such a ruckus, beating their drums and wailing to the heavens. There would be no peace until the heaven looked down upon them in disapproval, pushing them away. Nraug Hli's thoughts were disrupted as his favorite moment of each night appeared.

Along the horizon, a brightness began, her light chasing away the gloom of night. His hand automatically reaching for her as the first rays of light kissed his face. With an upturned face and sad smile, he slowly faded with the night.

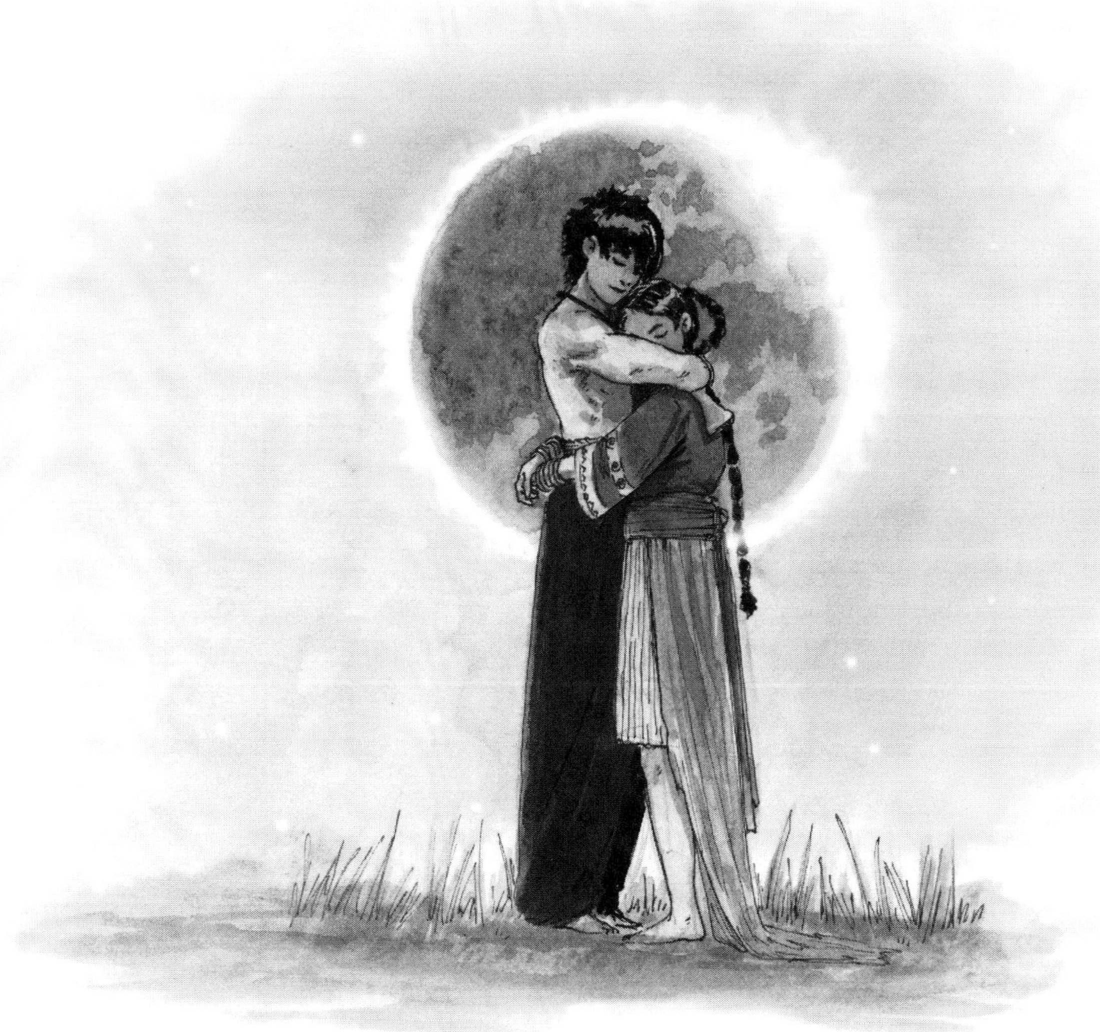

Emrace of the Sun and Moon

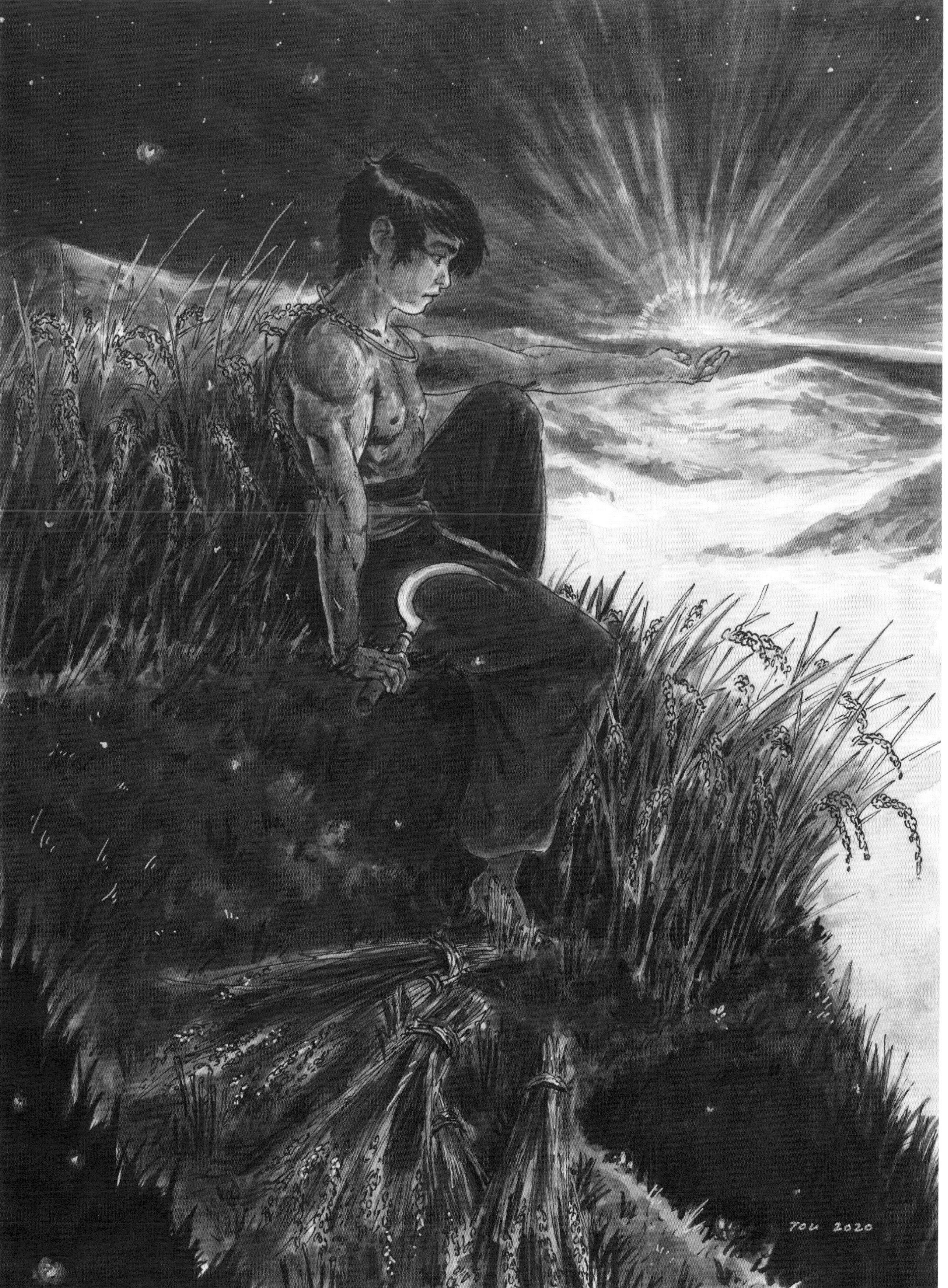
TOU 2020

Harvest

A long time ago, when the world was young, the heavens made life easy for the Hmong. When it was harvest time, ripened fruits and vegetables would go to the farmers' home. All he would have to do was build the storage unit to hold the food. This made life easy for the Hmong, until one harvest. A man decided to sleep instead of preparing for the crop to arrive.

When the harvest began to show up, they didn't know where to go, so they asked the man, "Have you built a storage space for us?"

The man woke from his slumber and saw the harvest was already there. Still groggy from his sleep, he replied, "I have not finished yet so you can go back to the fields. When I finish it, I will come and get you."

So, the harvest went back to the fields to await the farmer. That is why today, farmers have to work hard to prepare a place for the harvest and pick it from the fields.

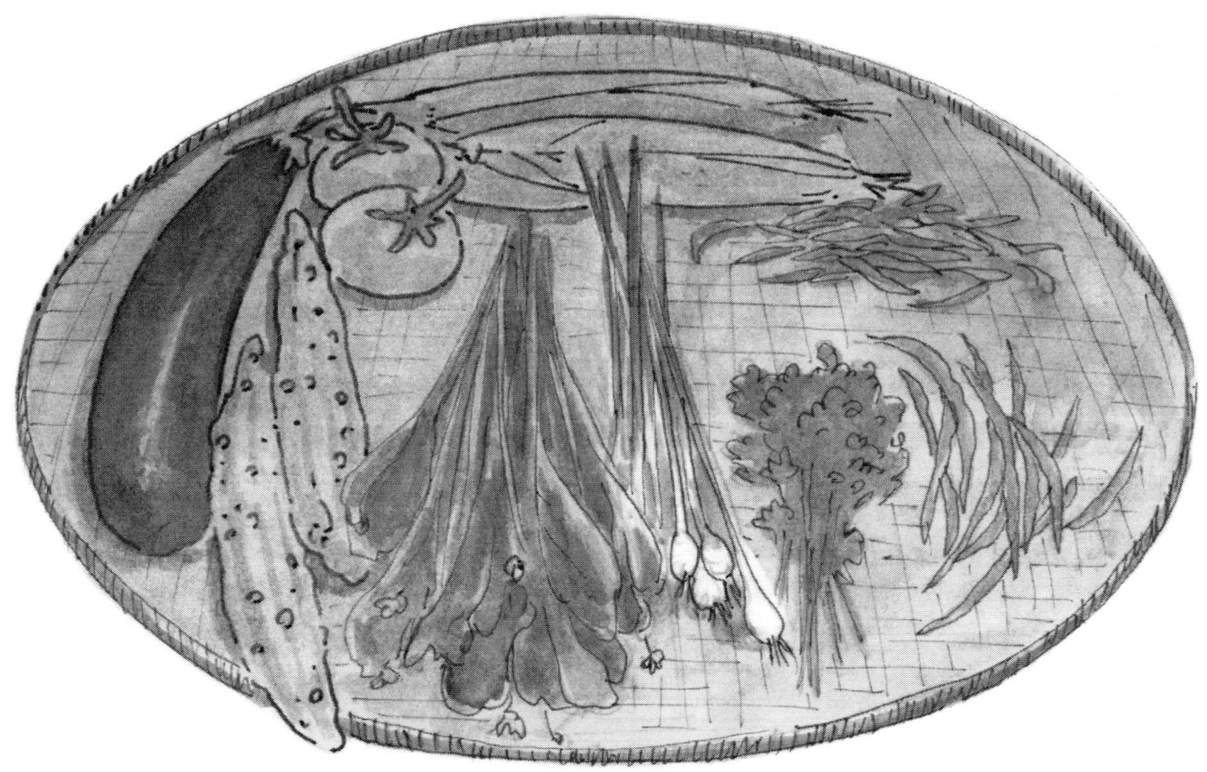

A gathering of crops on a Vab

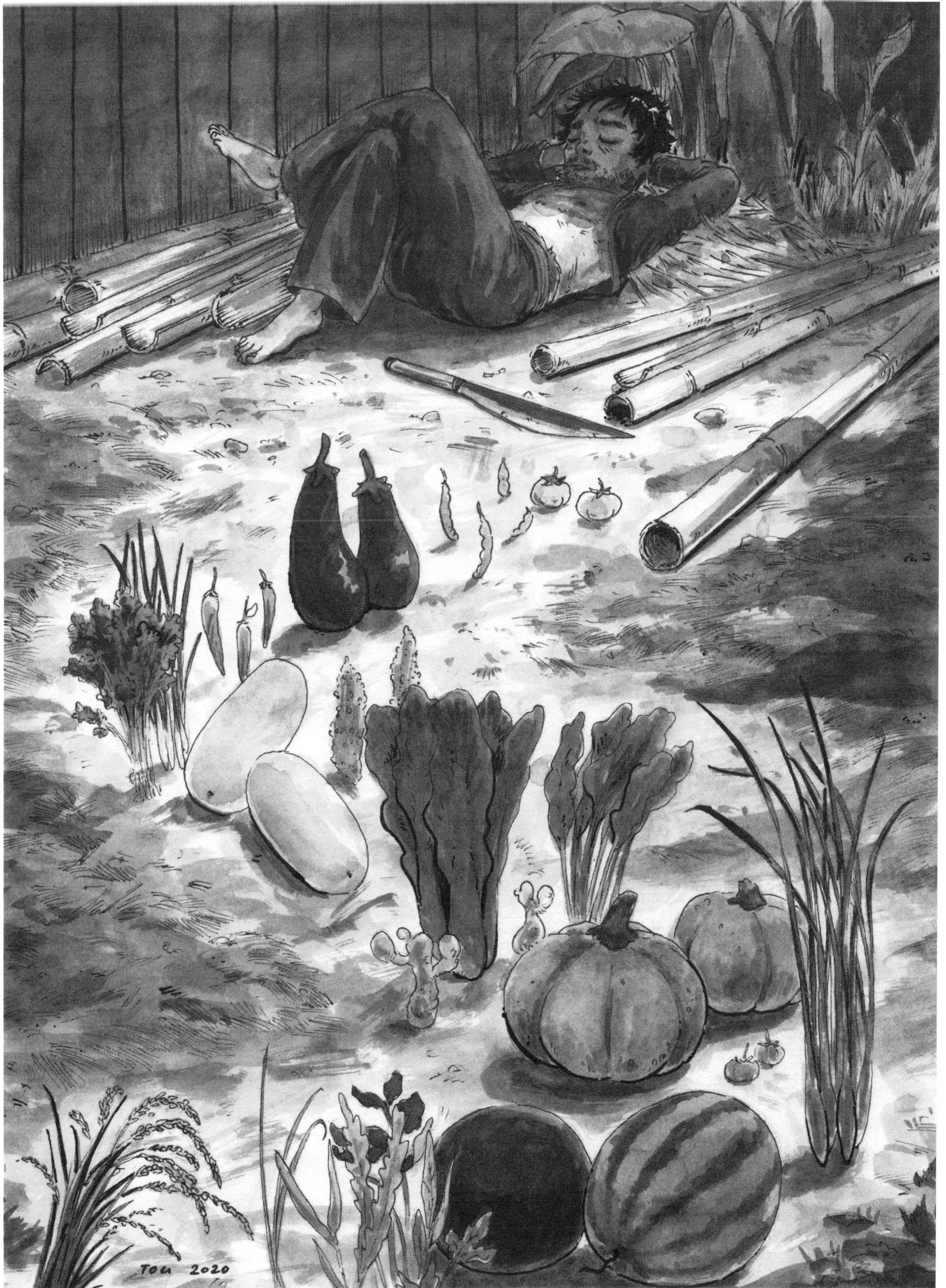
TOU 2020

Fog

Chi You is regarded by some as the Hmong King who led them against the Chinese armies in 26 BC. They fought over the fertile lands against the Yan and Yellow Emperor, the Han people's predecessor. Chi You was regarded as the Ox King and a god of war among his enemies due to his ferocity in battle. He won 9 major battles and 80 skirmishes against the Yellow Emperor. Only with the combined might of two imperial armies did Chi You's army lose the 10th battle.

With their advanced metal swords, Chi You was said to be a master swordsman that fought like a demon with eight arms. He commanded supernatural powers and could exude fog from his body to hide his army. Maybe this inspired the saying "fogs of war." Chi You's defeat was attributed to the Yellow Emperor, making a compass that helped him navigate the thick fog.

After his beheading on the field of battle, his three sons took the remaining people and split them apart. The eldest took his people south, and the middle son took his people north while the youngest stayed and assimilated into Chinese society. The Hmong people are descendants of the ones that went south and eventually ended up in South East Asia.

King Chiyou and the fog of war

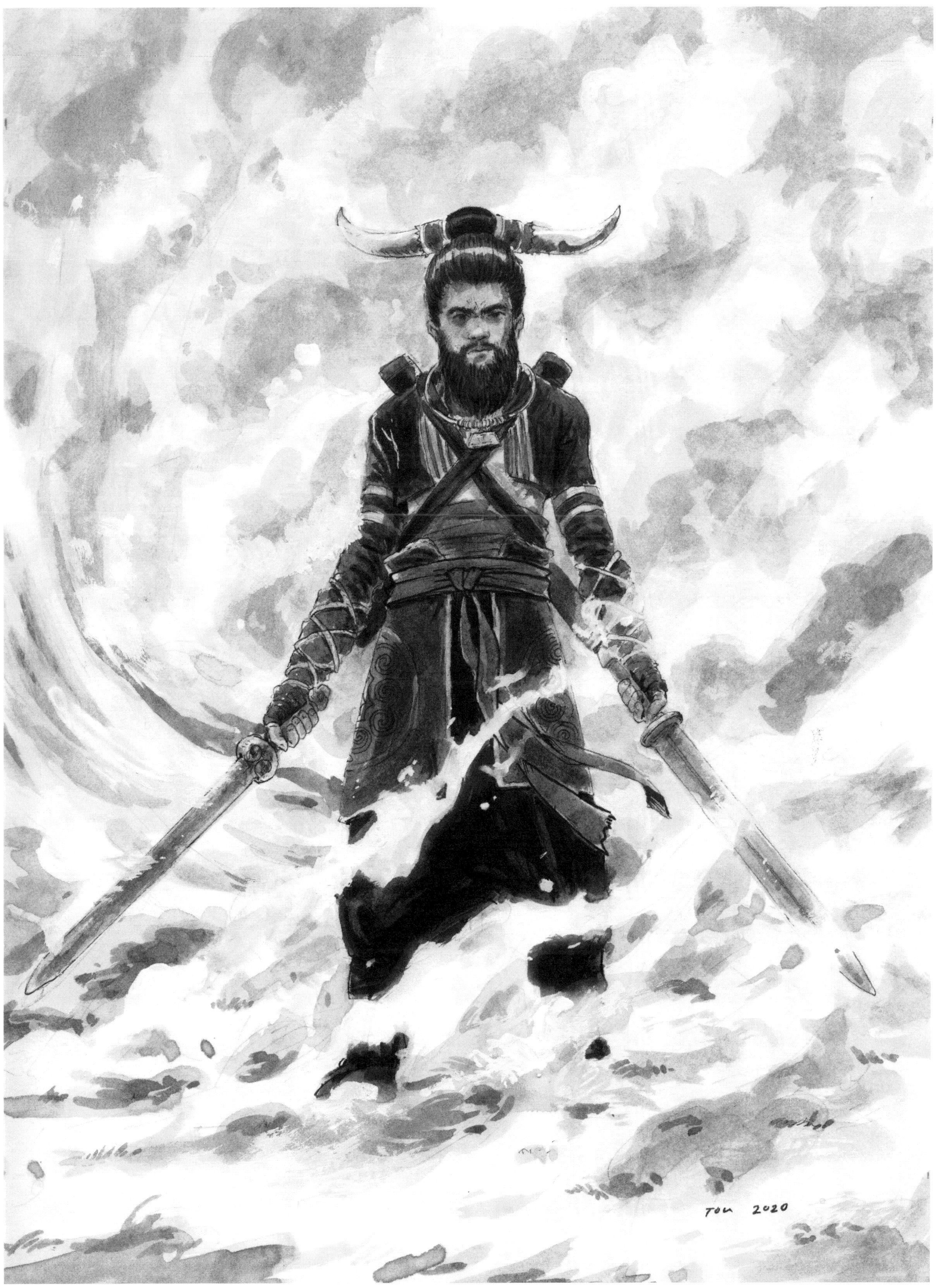
TOU 2020

Queen

For thousands of years, the Hmong have been in China. There have been countless years documenting the battles fought against the Chinese expansion. The Hmong were not the barbarians China claimed them to be. Instead, they were more advanced in some cases: rice cultivation, use of metal for swords, and archery. They had a kingdom led by Chi You who won many battles but lost the one that mattered.

His queen was a scholar who wanted to preserve the culture of her people. She knew that a purge was coming, and if no one preserved the knowledge collected by their people, they would be burned and forgotten. She ordered the women to sew the knowledge accumulated by their people onto the clothing they wore. They were to teach them to their children so that not all was lost.

She sent the people south to escape the fighting but stayed behind to rally the defenders. She hoped her people would find freedom and rise again from the fires like the phoenixes of legend.

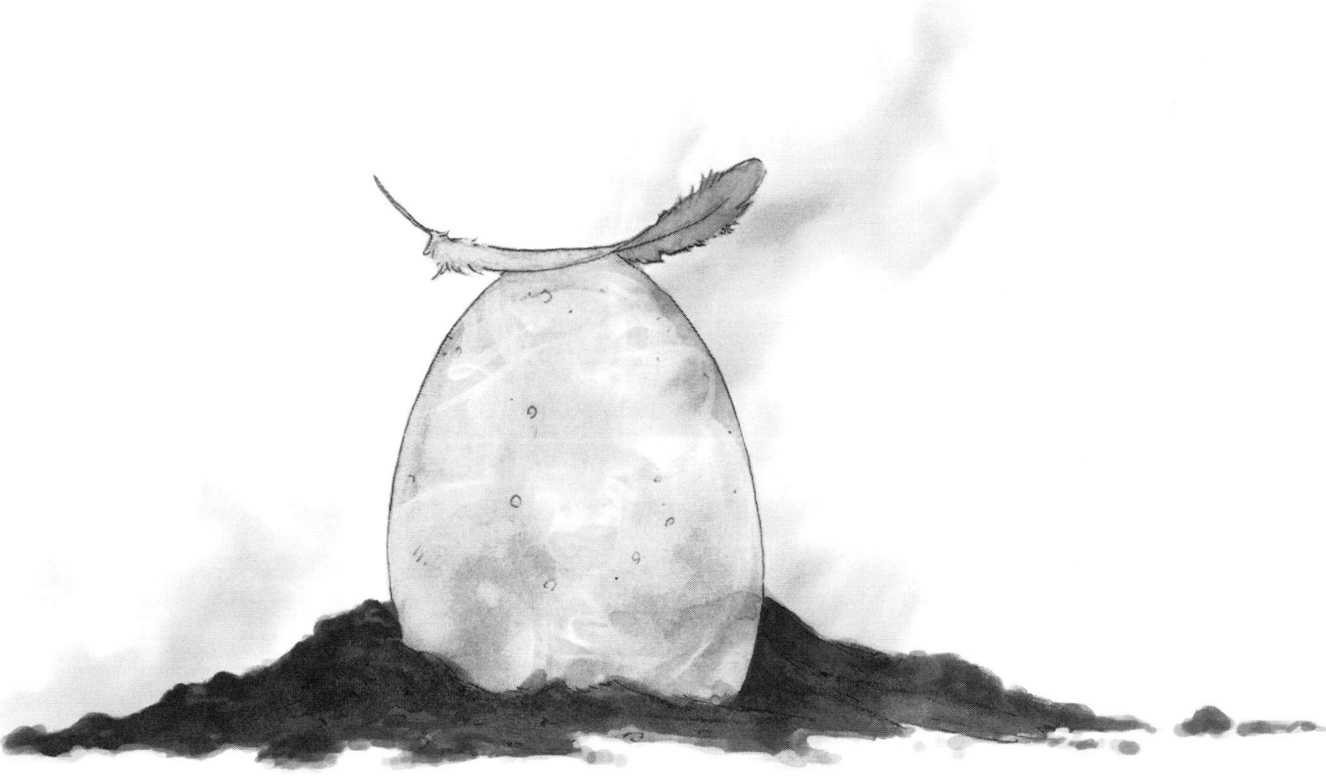

Phoenix egg ready for rebirth

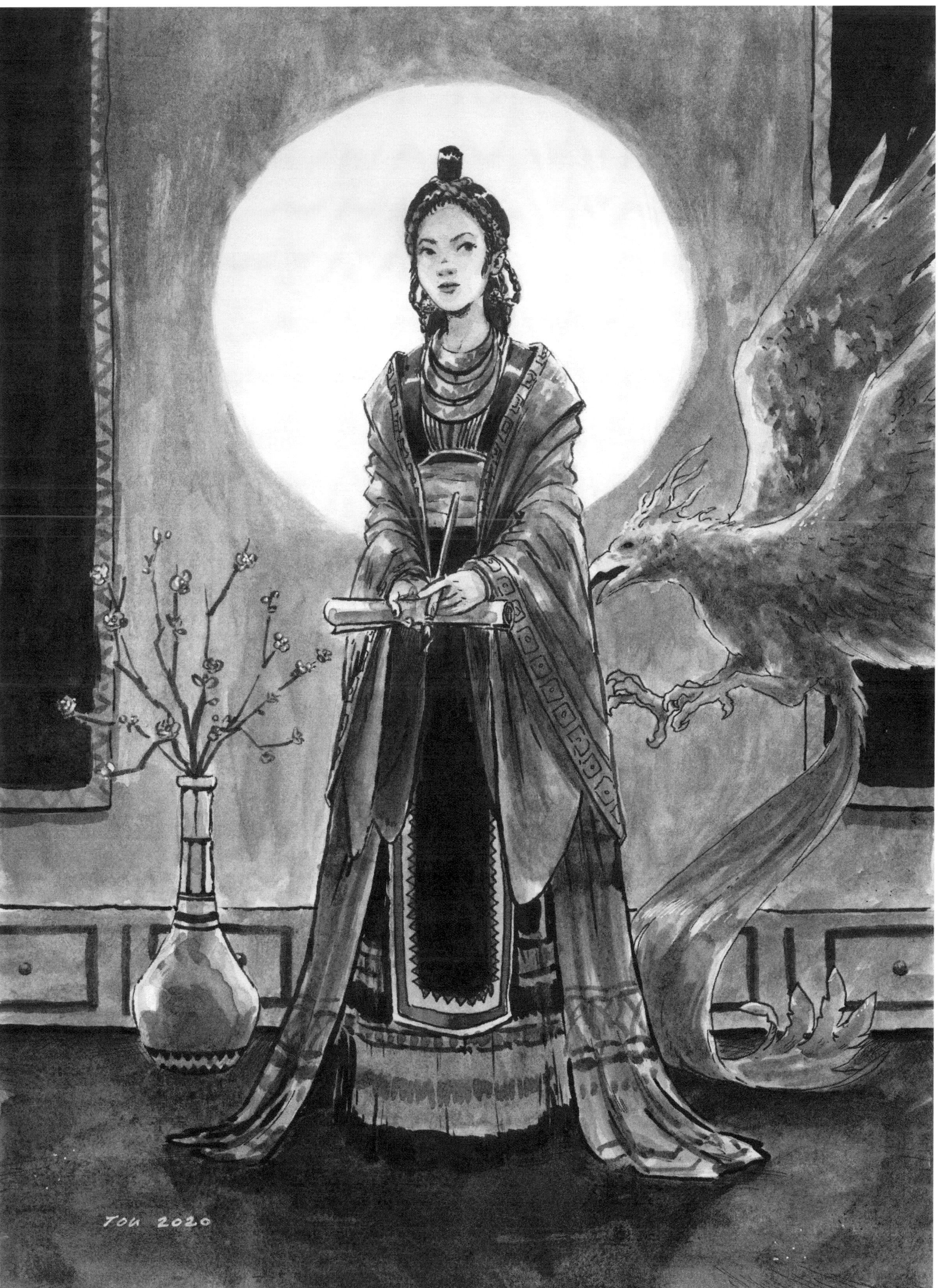
TOU 2020

Rain

Tub Ntsuag (orphan boy) was all alone in this world. His parents had died in a plague, and he had to go live with some distant relatives. They didn't care much for him, and there was no place for him in their tiny home. The only other place left for him was the farm shed on the mountainside.

Each night he would cry alone in the fields, remembering his parents who loved him. His tears moved the heavens, and they opened up and cried with him each night. The gentle pattering of suab naab, the voice of the rain, on the roof lulling him to peaceful sleep

With the constant rainfall over the fields he tended, Tub Ntsuag's crops were bountiful and grew bigger than the other villagers. His large harvest yields enabled him to support himself and bring face to his relatives. His position within the family grew, and he was able to catch the eye of a beautiful maiden. In honor of the rain that was his constant companion, he named his daughter Suab Naab, and he was never lonely again.

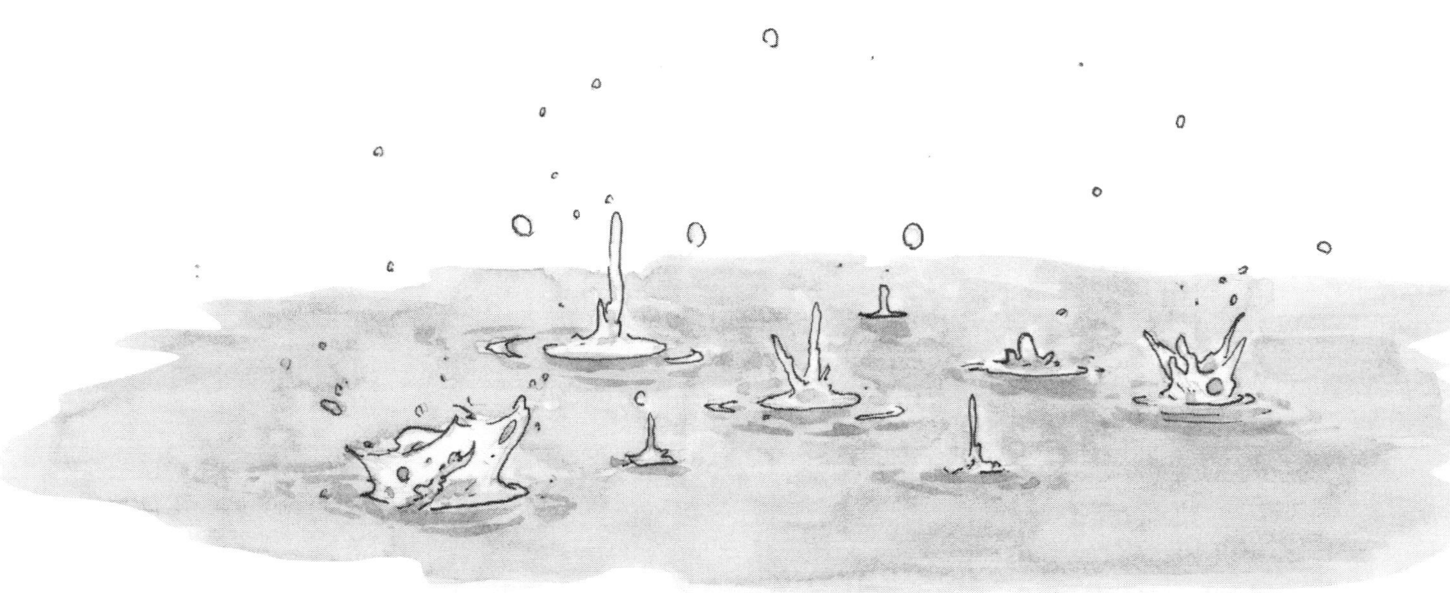

Gentle fall of rain

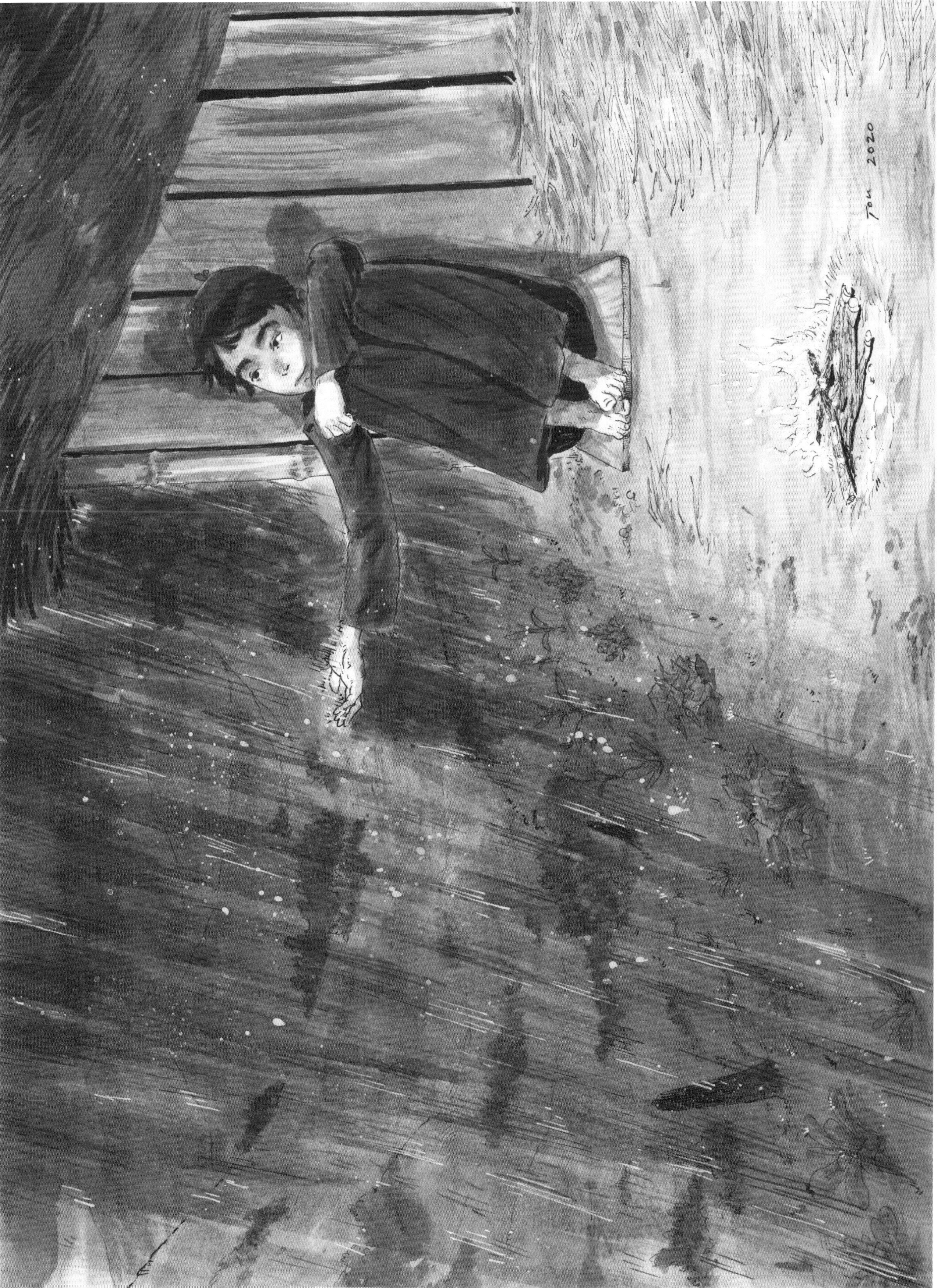

King

A long time ago, there was a man who wanted an audience with the King of Heaven. He traveled through fire and rain, ice-cold terrain, and scorching heat. Through it all, he suffered until finally, he found the Kings' palace. Little did he know, all mortals were to be killed on sight. Only his quick feet saved him from the arrows fired upon him at the palace gates. After a narrow escape from the guards, he found a passage through the bathing area.

There he saw the seven daughters of the King and made a change to his plan. He decided to kidnap the eldest daughter instead and make the King come to him. He grabbed her while she was washing her hair and quickly tied her hands and feet. He carried her out of the palace grounds, but her screams had already captured the attention of her sisters, who called for the King.

With the guards trailing his steps, the man fled with the princess back through the fiery and cold lands. The King of Heaven called forth the beasts and animals to help him, and they slowed the man's journey with attacks. Wounded and near death, the man almost succumbed to his pain, but the kind-hearted princess took care of him and nursed him back to health. After waking up, he fell in love with her and decided to keep her for his own. To keep her, all he would have to do was take her to his home and make her his bride.

When he reached his home, he yelled to his father that he had brought home a bride. His father grabbed a chicken, swept it over their heads to tie their spirits together, and call her spirit to her new home. After the ritual was complete, she was bound to him. The clouds darkened the sky as lightning flashed and thunder roared. The heavens anger could be felt, but there was nothing he could do to bring back his daughter.

The King's only alternative to protect his remaining children was to sunder the way to his kingdom. He closed off the path to heaven from mortals forever.

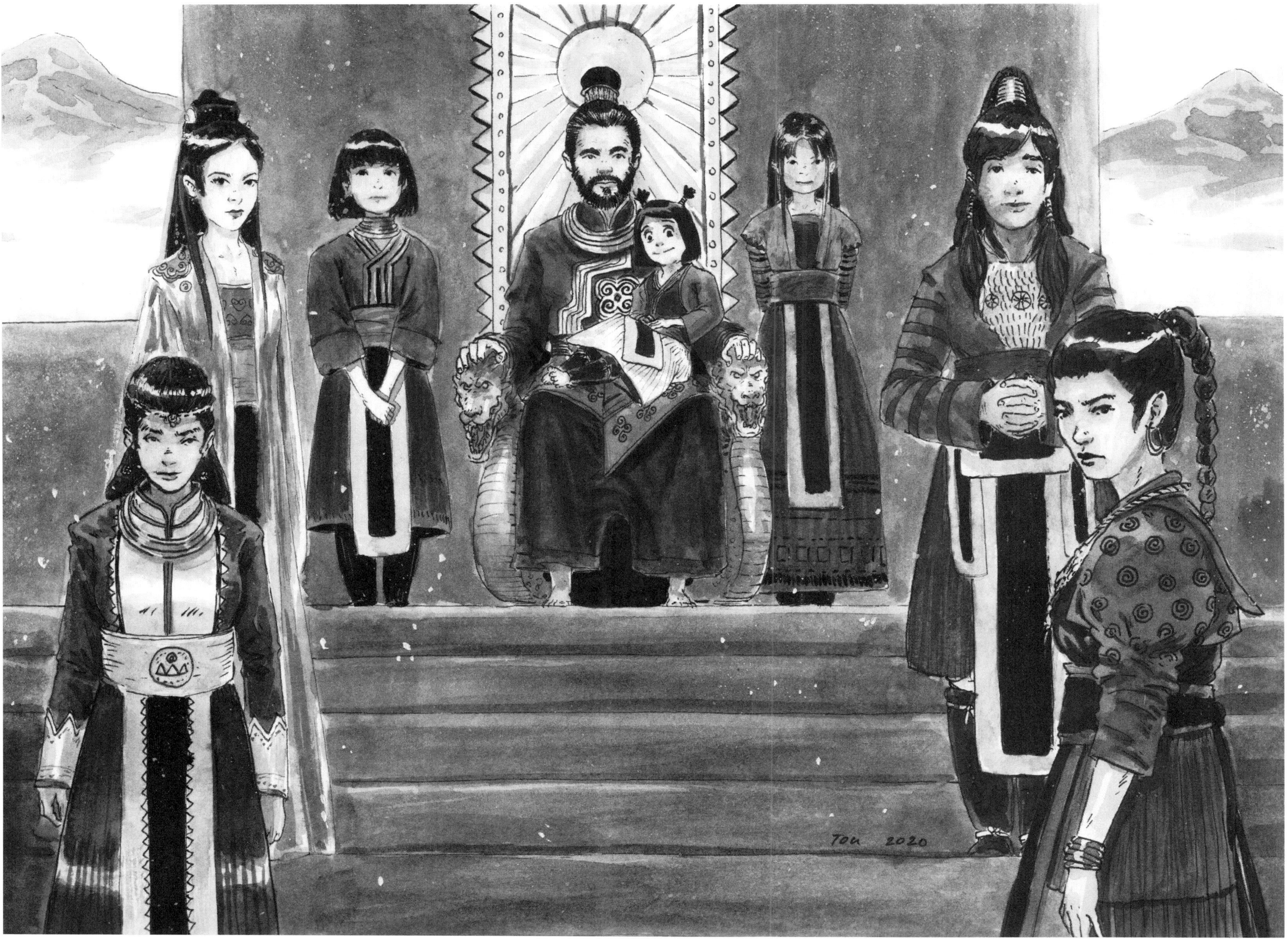
Tou 2020

Umbrella

The day was getting late when the children left Grandma's house. She had beseeched them to spend the night, but they adamantly refused. She gave them an umbrella and said if they felt scared, open the umbrella up, and it will hide them.

As the children were walking home, darkness descended faster in the jungle, and the night animals started to wander around for food. Each sound startled the kids and made them jump. The small ones started to cling onto Nkauj Jou as they peered into the dark.

Suddenly the hairs stood straight up on the back of their necks, and a shiver ran down their bodies. Something was following them. Quickly, Nkauj Jou opened the umbrella, and they all squeezed under it. Not a moment later, a sniffling shambling figure walked by them, seeking their scent. Now the children wished they had stayed at Grandma's as they watched the figure pass by.

Onward they pushed, underneath the umbrella, invisible to the spirits. Next to the trail stood two trees that were not there earlier. Where did they come from? Whoosh, the wind pushed past them as they noticed a giant hand grabbing an animal in the under-brush. It was Mos Hlub who had set an ambush. The children screamed and ran away while Mos Hlub was busy looking at the sky, and they escaped the monster. They reached home all out of breath and vowed never to go out after dark again without an umbrella.

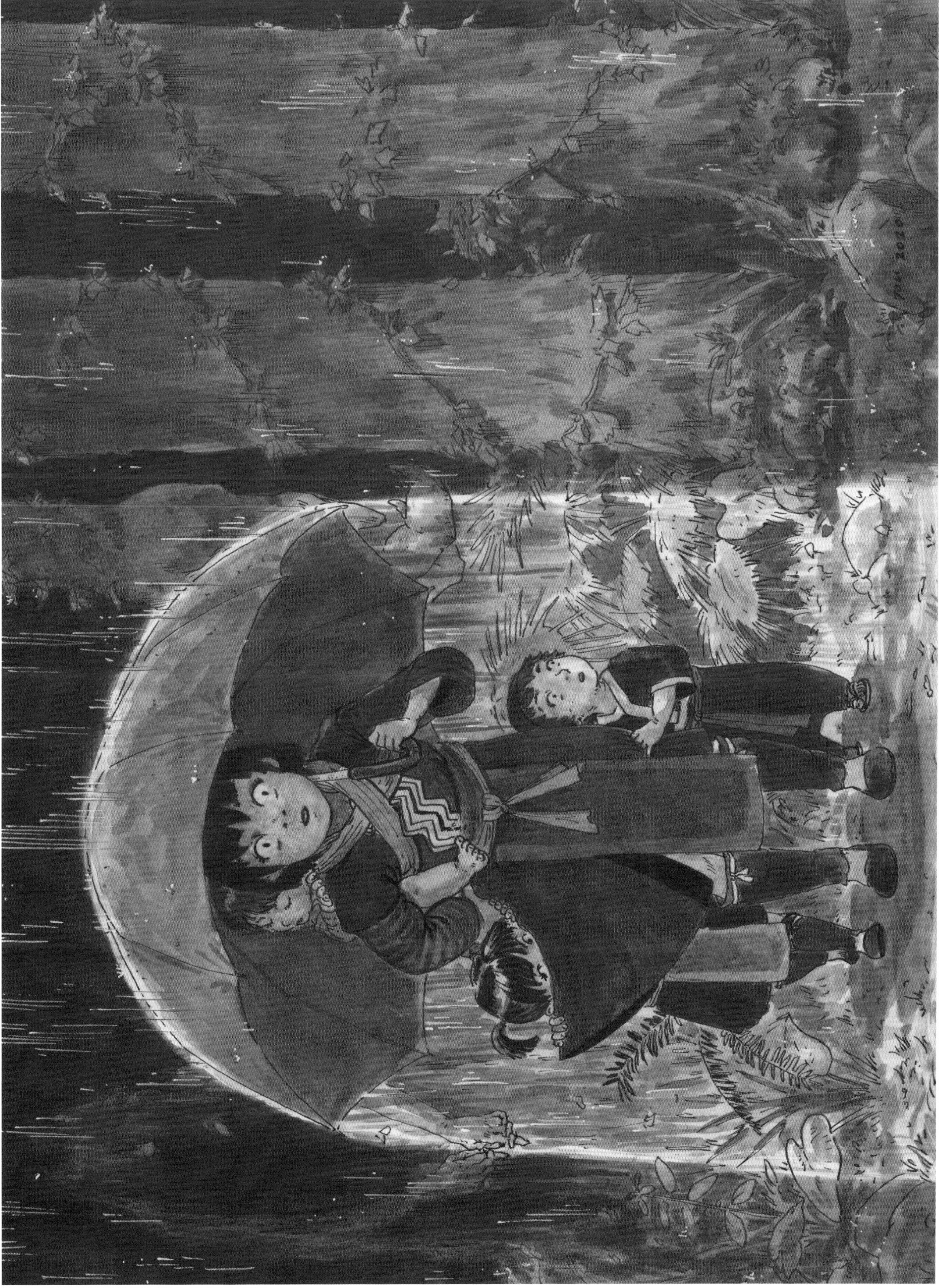

Dragon

A long time ago, a boy fell in the river and was beyond saving. His family cried to the heavens for help, but they quickly lost hope as the current swept the boy downstream. The family ran along the river bank, hoping that he would somehow make it out. Then suddenly, the river swelled up, and a dragon burst forth carrying the boy.

The people screamed in fright, thinking that the dragon was evil, the people began to throw rocks at him. Blinded by their fear, a rock was thrown true and struck the dragon's snout. It became angry that the little pests had thought to drive him away after he rescued the boy.

With a deafening roar, he splashed the people with a huge wave. Instead of delivering the boy to shore, it curled tightly around the boy's body anddove into the depths of the river. The boy was never seen again.

A dragon's enmity is eternal, and his anger knew no bounds. He vowed to take any human he sees near a riverbank and even convinced all dragons to do the same.

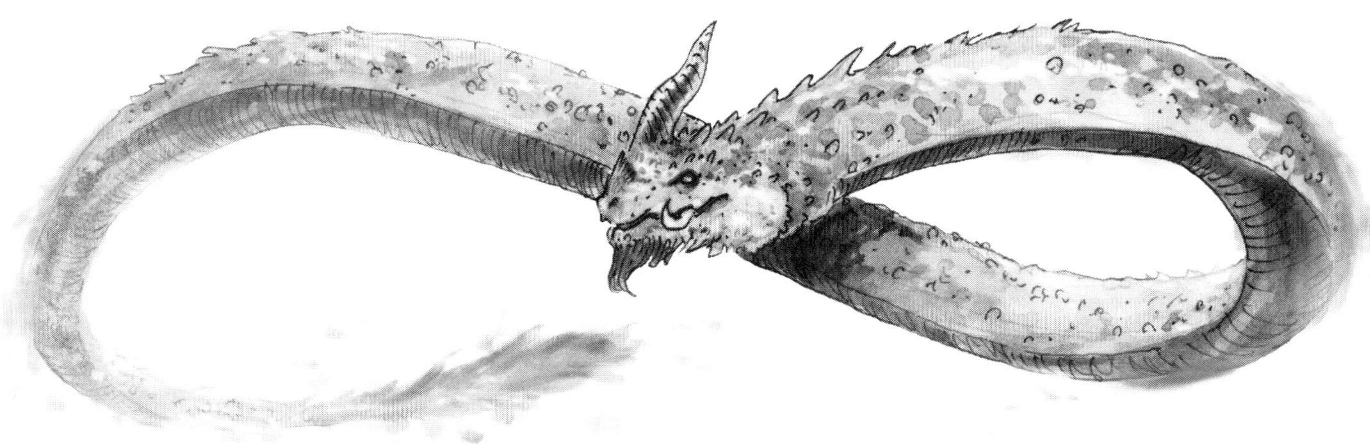

The infinite ire of a dragon

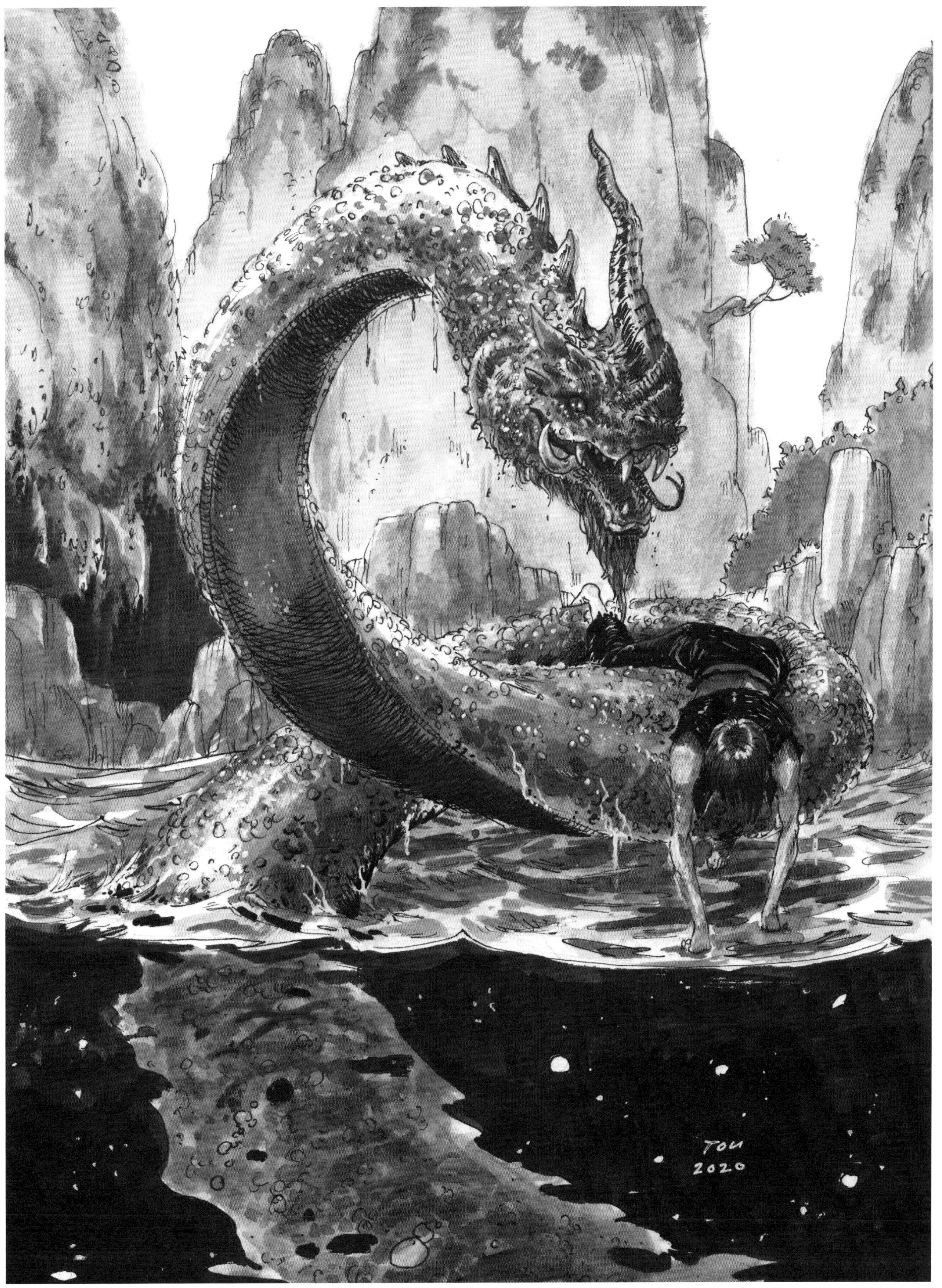
TOU
2020

The Hmong are superstitious people and believed that cats were a bad omen. The smaller cousins of tigers and Tswv Xyas (first tiger spirit) would use them as carriers of his minions, the puj ntxoog. If a cat crossed the threshold of your home, it meant that sickness was going to strike a family member, even death may occur. For this reason, cats were always chased from villages and were never domesticated. Many families kept dogs around to chase cats away.

Growing up, my sister brought home a kitten, and my mom threw a fit. She said the kitten had to go because it was bad luck. Even away from Laos, she carried this superstition with her.

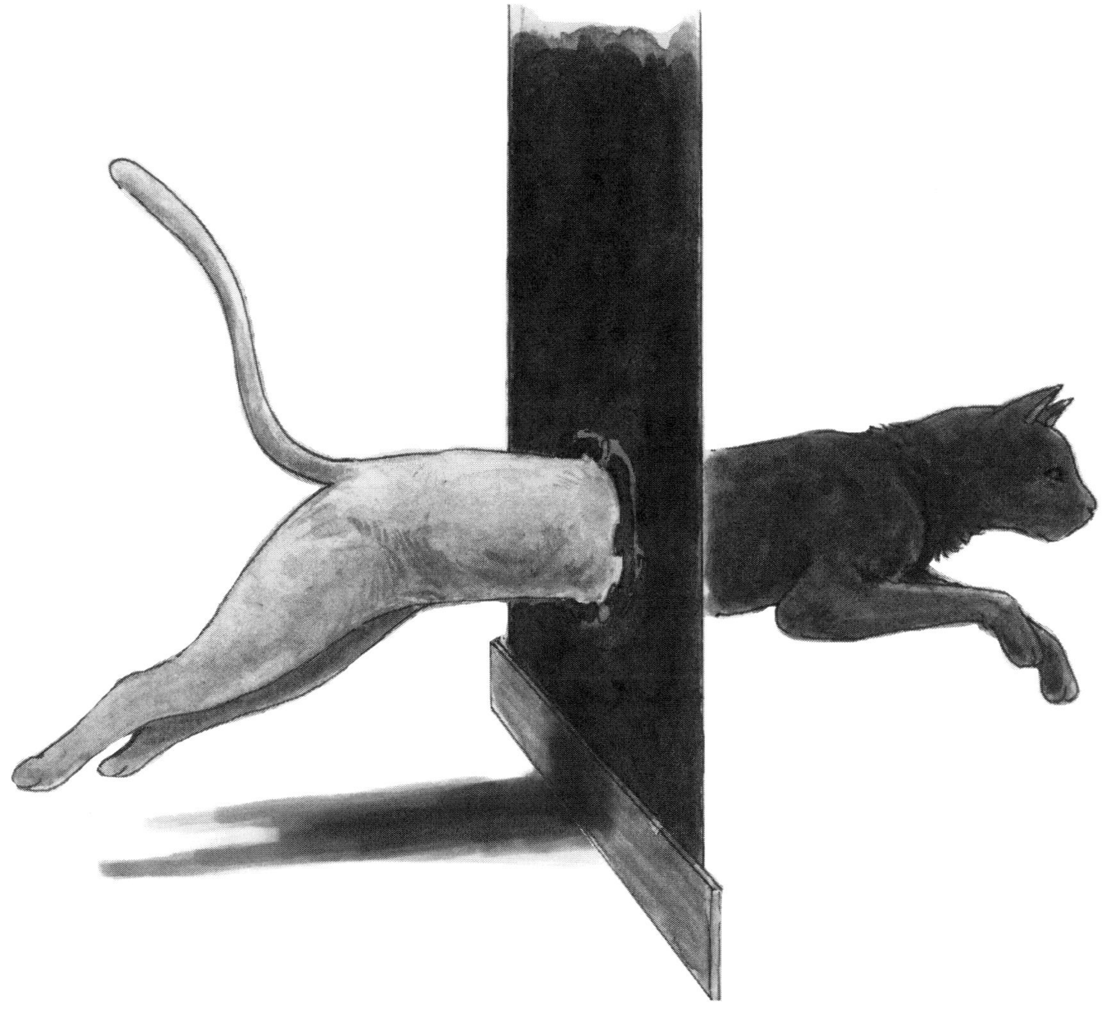

A cat crossing the threshold

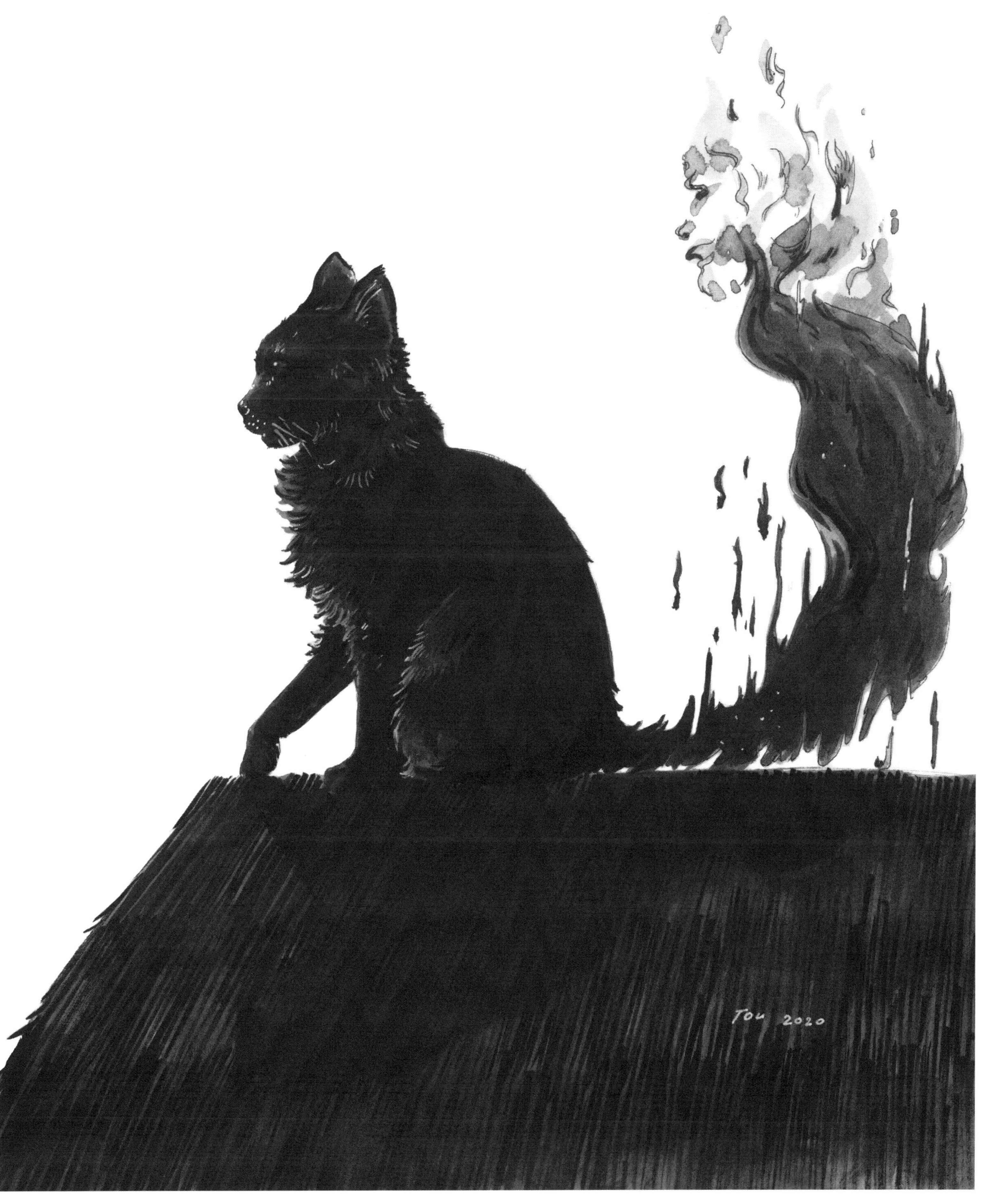
TOU 2020

Tiger

For two years, Nuj Nplhaib had tracked the Tiger Lord to find his girl Ntxawm (Yer). She was taken from him when a spiteful admirer called out loud that she was the prettiest girl on the whole mountain. This proclamation caused the malicious spirits to inform the Tiger Lord, who collected the best among humanity. One evening while going home from the fields, the Tiger Lord and his minions ambushed and carried her off.

Everyone had told him to move on and forget about her. No one had ever succeeded in rescuing someone kidnapped by the tigers. His love for her led him to journey through mountains and treacherous lands to bring her back. He told his family to think of him as dead since he would not return without her by his side. In the beginning, his naivety and lack of skill almost got him killed a few times. Remembering his luck made him smile. His skill at arms and spells increased with each victory against the spirits and minions that blocked his way. He had lost friends and made more enemies in his search for Ntxawm.

A break in the clouds revealed the Tiger Lord and Ntxawm atop the rocky overhang. A tiger leapt out of the bushes. With a quick sidestep and a powerful slash with his sword, Nuj Nplhaib severed its head. Another growl from behind made him roll to the side, barely dodging a massive paw. Midroll, he threw out an energy ball that exploded against the tigresses' side. With a mighty roar, the Tiger Lord summoned the rest of his minions. As demons, tigers, and spirits surrounded him, he stood up with a mad grin and flicked the bloody sword clean. The final battle had begun.

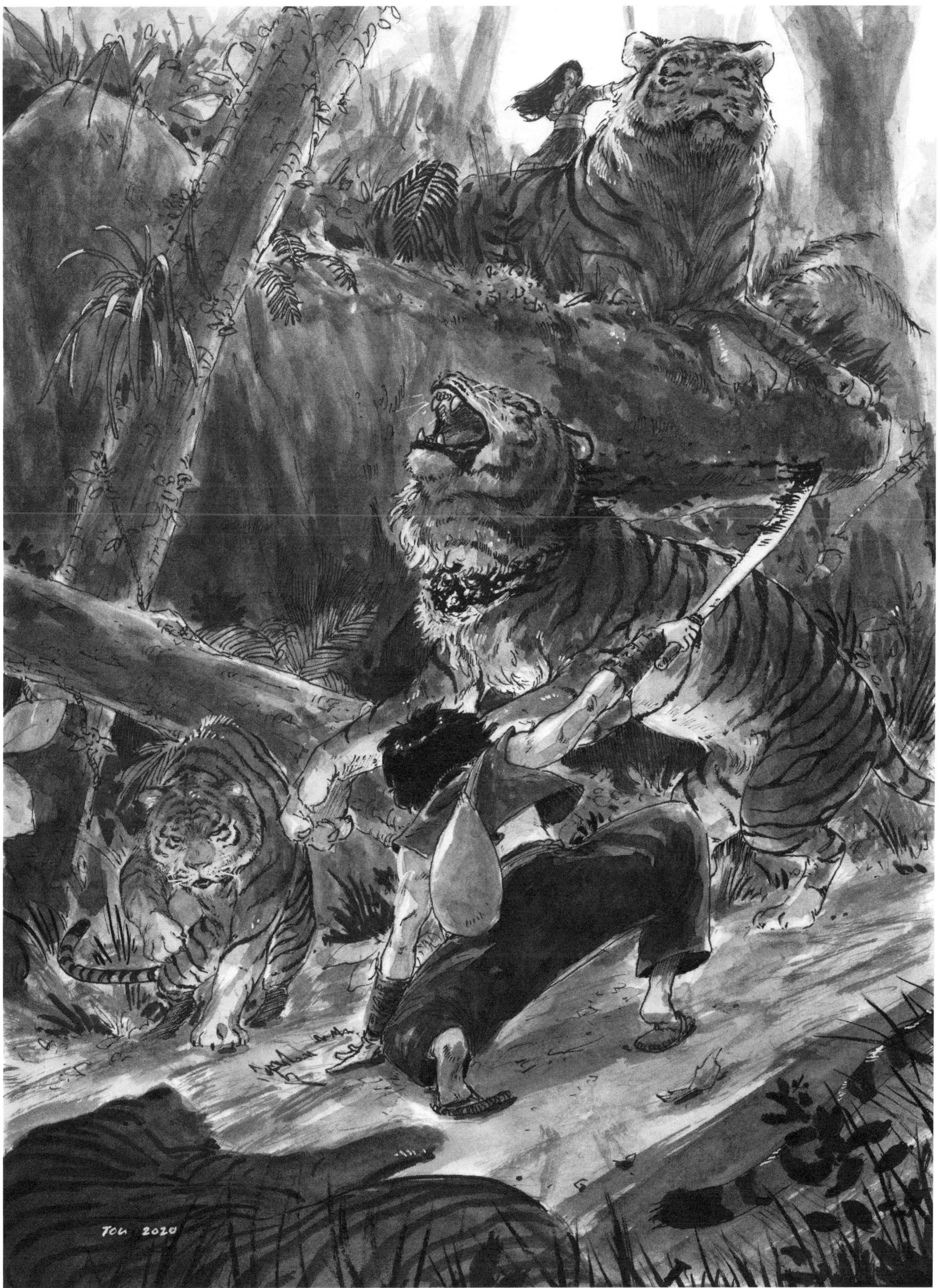
TOU 2020

Ghost

As the sun sets, the Hmong village began to turn down for the night. Doors that are opened all day were now closed, and the fires banked. The chickens and dogs had settled in and sleeping soundly. The young and adventurous men snuck around the village to talk to the girls. A light scratch and whispers in the dark were all it took to start the flirting. Little did some of these girls know, not all the conversations were with the living.

Soon, the village girls started to disappear. One by one, the families would awaken to find the girls were gone. Their clothes and shoes were still by their bedside, and the door was still latched. After questioning the siblings, the villagers knew what had happened.

So the word spread from village to village, mountain to mountain. When girls hear the scratching of the wooden walls and whispers asking to talk, they had to ask the question, "Are you living, or are you a ghost?" (Koj yog neej los koj yog dlaab?)

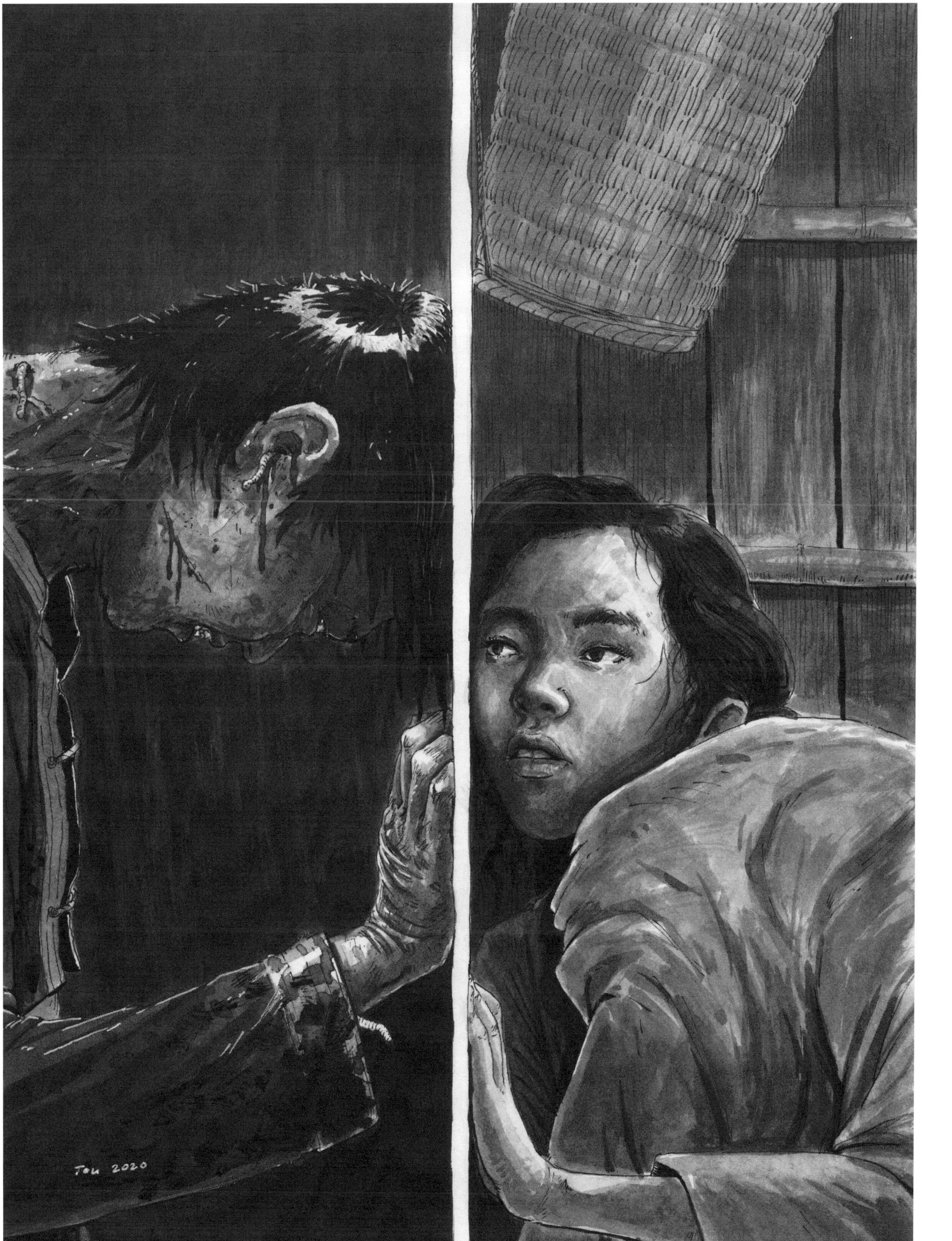

Tou 2020

Curse

A long time ago, there was a couple that loved each other. They had a few children to fill up the house. One day the wife unexpectedly fell ill and was bedridden for years. The husband grew to resent her and started to beat her and would yell at her about the smallest things. He wanted to set her aside and marry a second wife. She was heartbroken, and over time her heart too began to change.

One day during a drunken night, his mood darkened, and he beat her to death's door. She cursed him and their life together and said she would never let him go. Even death could not hold her bitterness and anger. She cursed him and vowed to come back as a tiger spirit and torment him. As she uttered the last words, the breath left her body, and she died.

The husband was scared of her words and told the children to gather the village and his cousins. Soon the home was filled with their neighbors. The women of the village prepared her body for burial, and after three days of funeral rites, they took her body and buried it in the forest. As they carried her body, the pallbearers soon noticed that the body had started to twitch. The gloom of the forest and the coming evening made them rush to the burial spot, and in their haste, they dumped her body in the hole and ran back to the village.

No sooner had the husband and relatives ran into his home, a thwomp was heard on his roof. They clearly heard shuffling and sniffling from above. Screams filled the home, and the children wailed, "Dad, Mom went to become a tiger and is back for you."

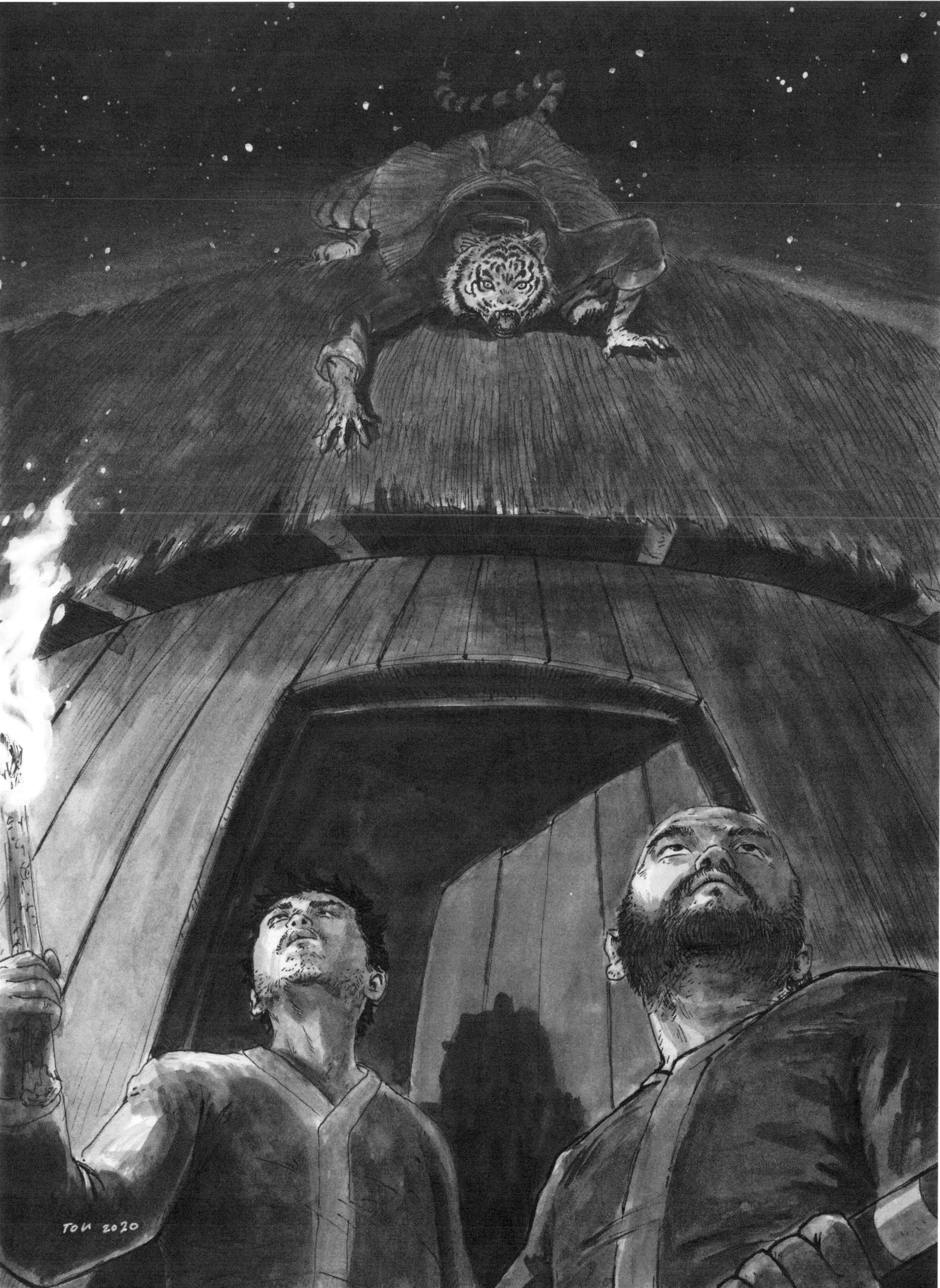
TOU 2020

HISTORY

The History of the Hmong is a long a winding one. From the hills of China to the lands of South East Asia, the Hmong have lived apart from the indigenous people.They preferred the freedom of the mountains despite the hardship of life there. They lived a rugged life akin tothe Highland people of Scotland and loved fiercely the life that was their own. Here is a glimpse into the life of the Hmong people andthe struggles they faced in the old country and life abroad.

Mountain

"...beeebee..boooboo..buueeee..." drifted the sound of the lonely boy atop the mountain. His leaf music speaks of his longing to see his girlfriend. The trip to see her would take a day and a night, across three valleys and two mountains. Life above the cloud line is challenging, but it is the only way to remain a free people.

The Hmong language is considered to be one of the most musical in the world. It can easily be replicated with music because it uses eight tones. If you have an ear for music, you will love the tonal Hmong language. It is a difficult language to pick up since each word can have multiple meanings depending on how you say it.

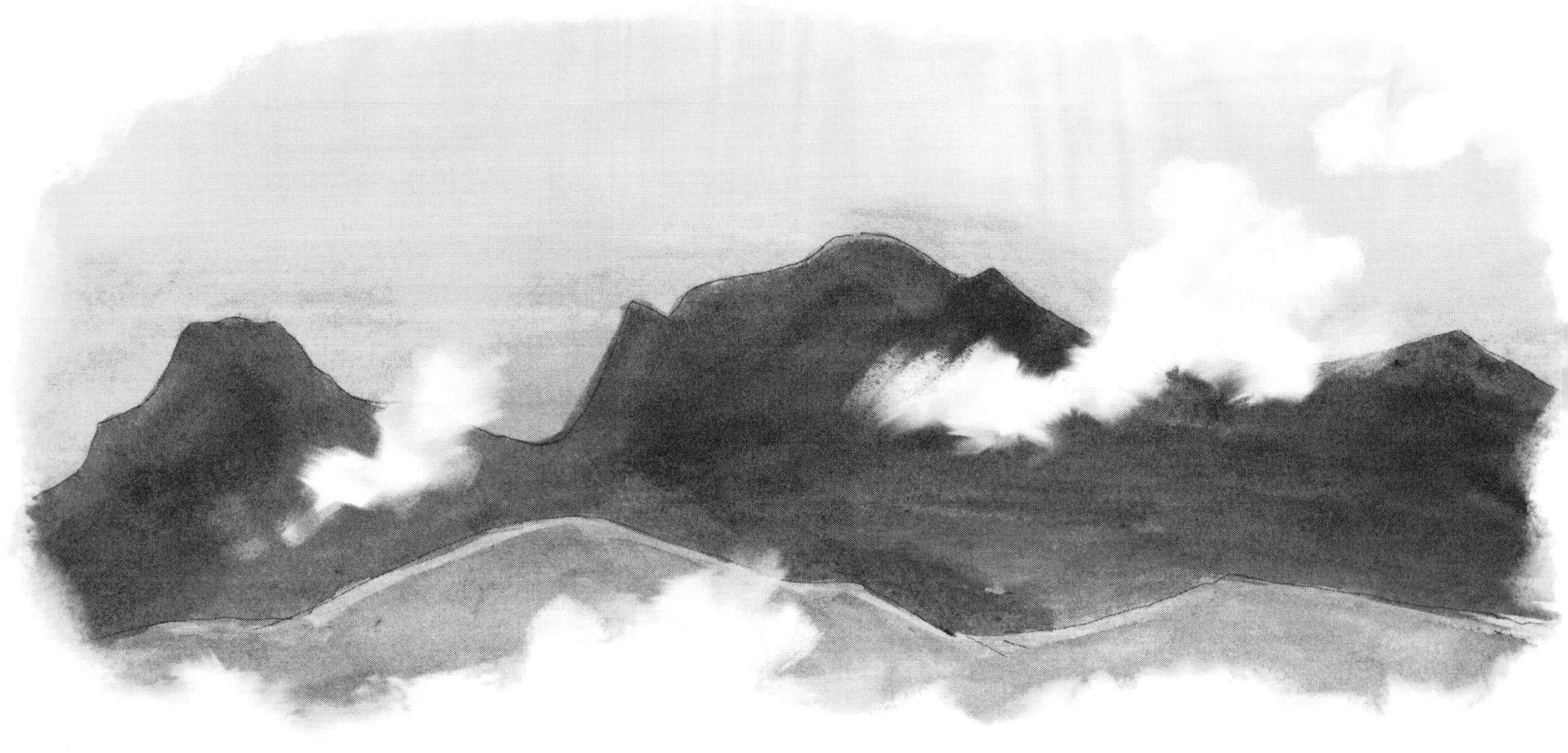

Mountains of Laos

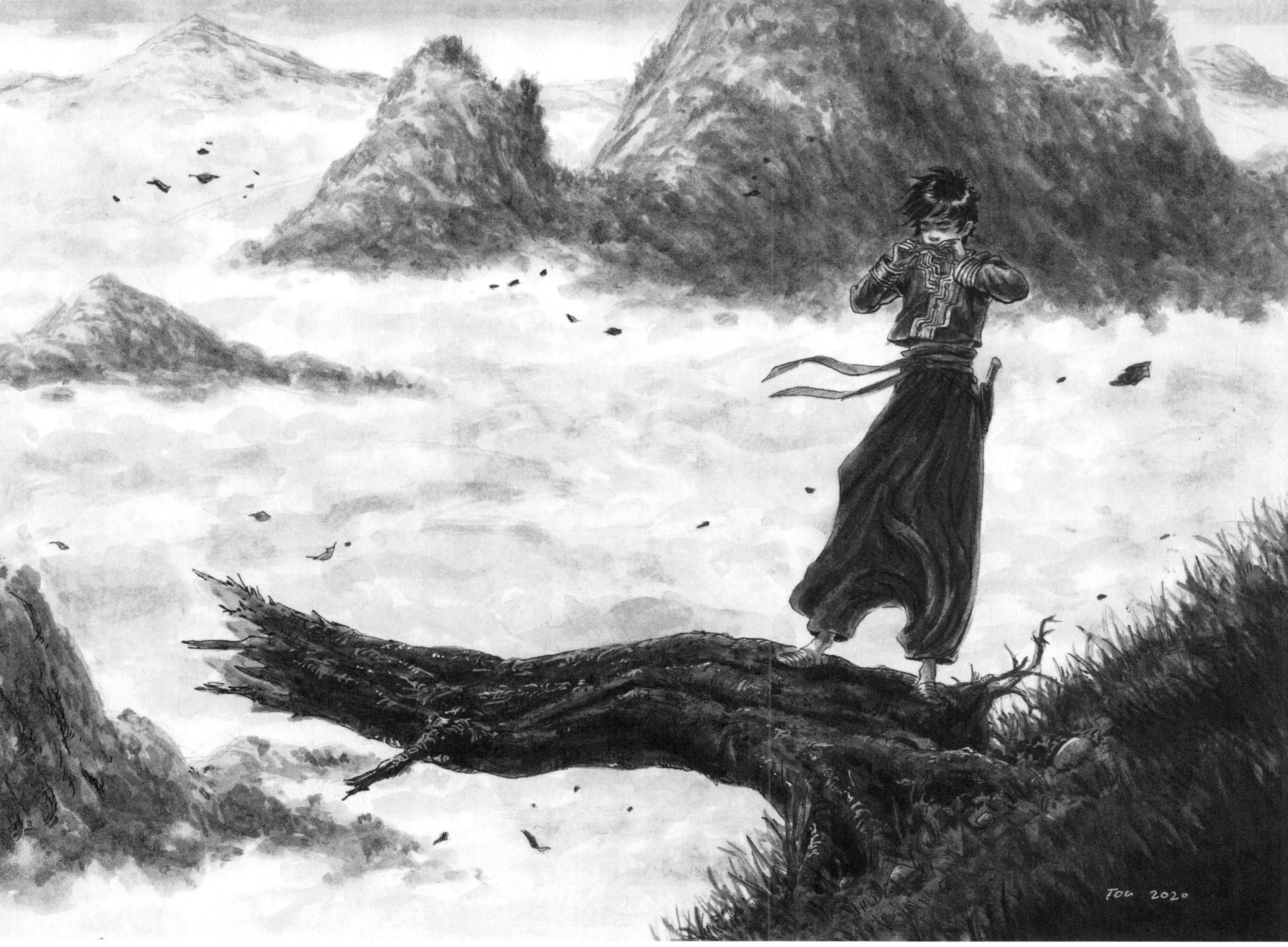
Tou 2020

The Hluas Nkauj zoo Nkauj (beautiful young girl) had just finished collecting firewood for the day. She was walking up the mountain when the wind blew by and carried the song of her love to her. She recognized his voice through the music of the blown leaf. Excitingly, she pulled out her ncaas (jaw/Jew harp) and played a response to her love "...twaaaanngg...twaaa...twaaaaannn..."

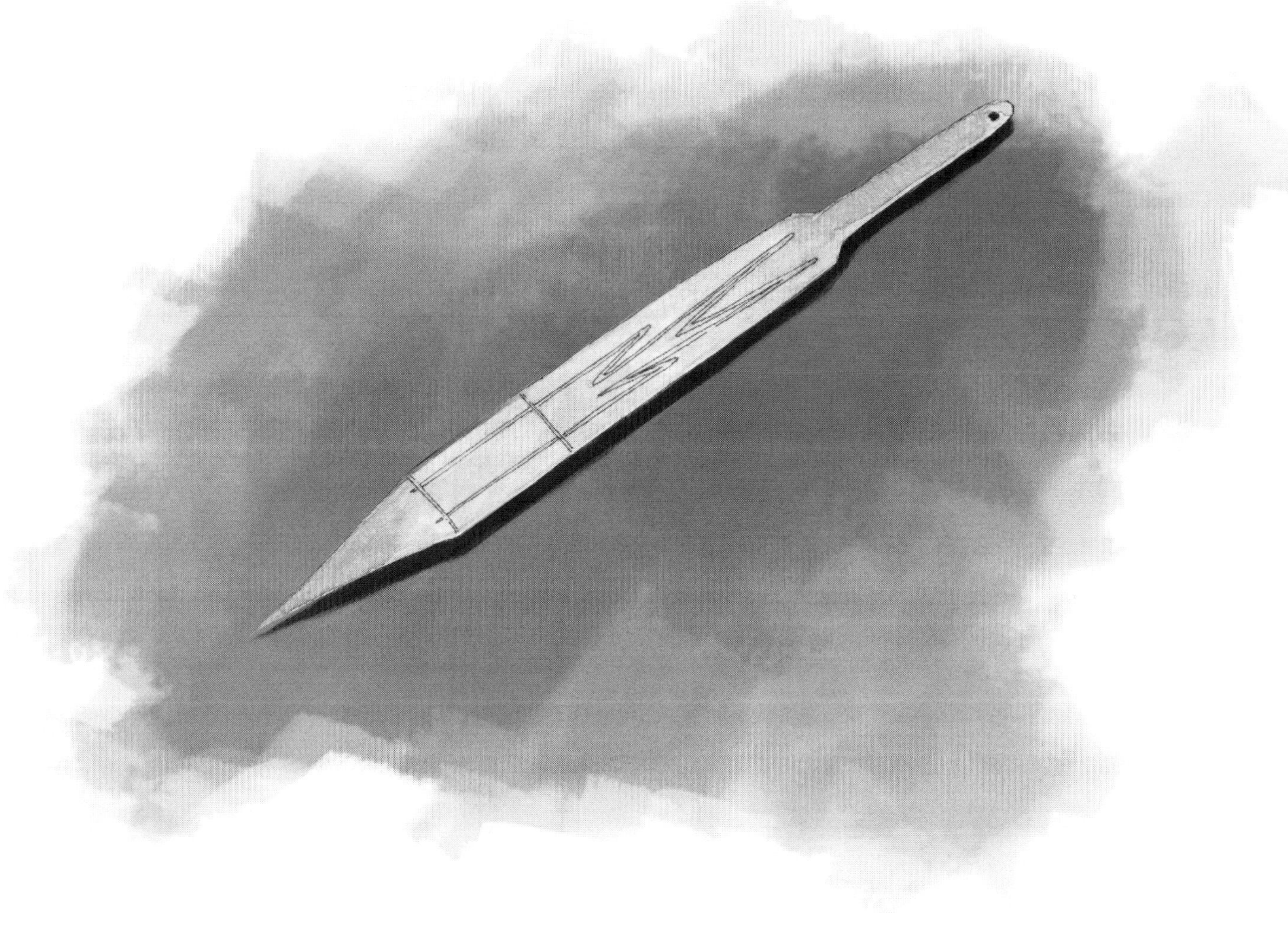

Close up of a Hmong ncaas

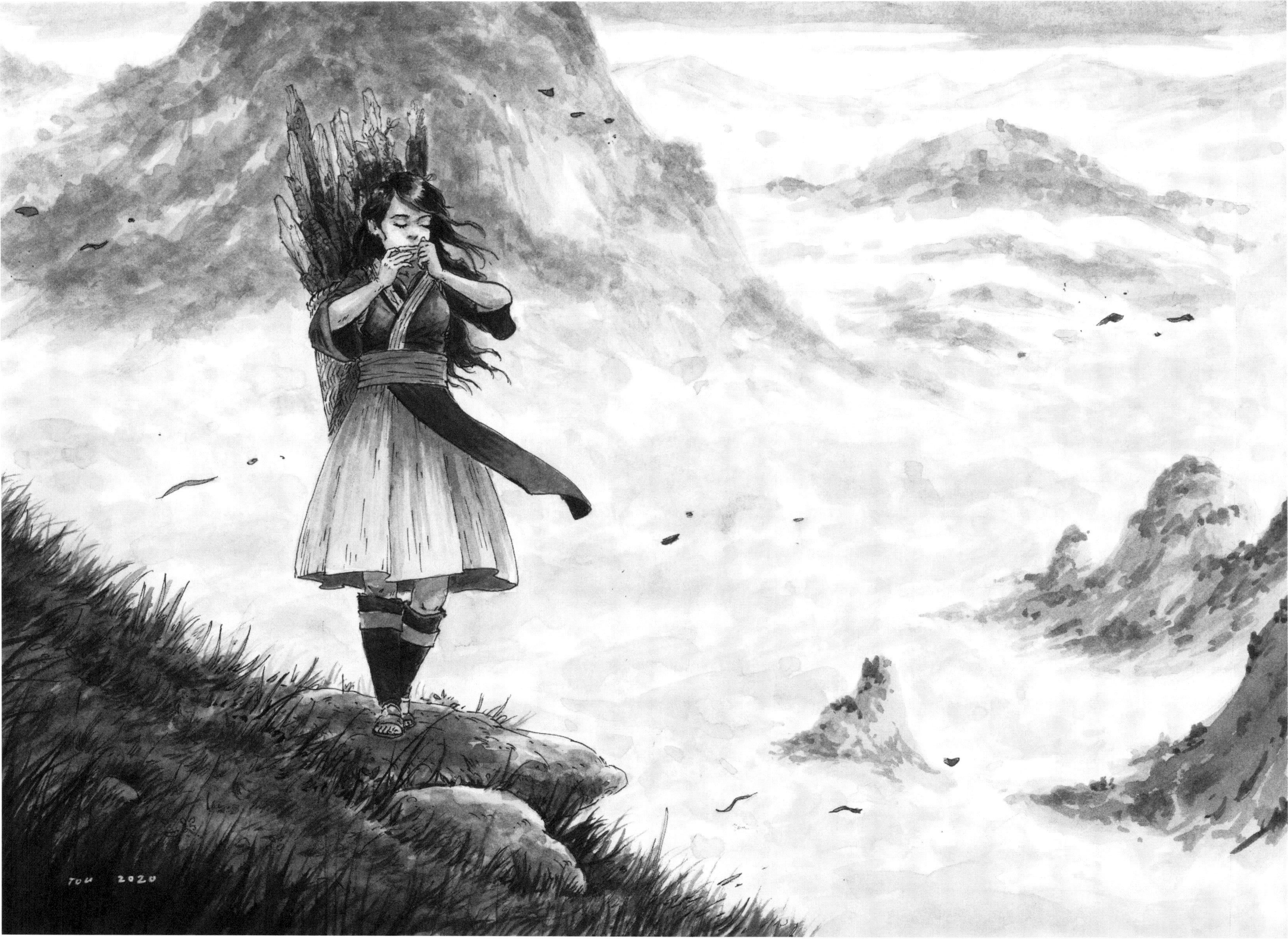
TOU 2020

Authentic Hmong fabric was made using fibers from the hemp plant. To achieve a full outfit, it would take a dedicated girl about a year to complete, just in time for the new year celebrations. It was every girls dream to make a new outfit to show off but few achieved to make one every year. It was easier to buy fabric and dye from the city, but for the poor families, making it from scratch was the only way. Most times, it was only the girl who would put in the work to make her own future.

All this laborious work was done by hand without the aid of any machinery. Making fabric consisted of cutting down the hemp plant, stripping the stalk of leaves, and then peeling the stalk into fine strands. Afterward, the strands would be pounded to soften the hemp, making it easier to twist into one continuous string. The strings would then be transferred onto a spindle and then combined to make a larger strand ready to be boiled and washed for three days.

To turn the string into cloth, the girls would use a loom to make a fine weave of hemp fabric. The fabric would then be boiled again with ash, roots, or berries to make indigo or black color that is the trademark of Hmong clothes. She would then cut the fabric down and start the needle working process to design the patterns that will adorn her clothes. You can always see the girls doing paaj ntaub on their downtime to complete their outfits in time for the New Year celebration.

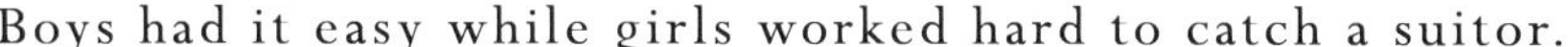

Boys had it easy while girls worked hard to catch a suitor.

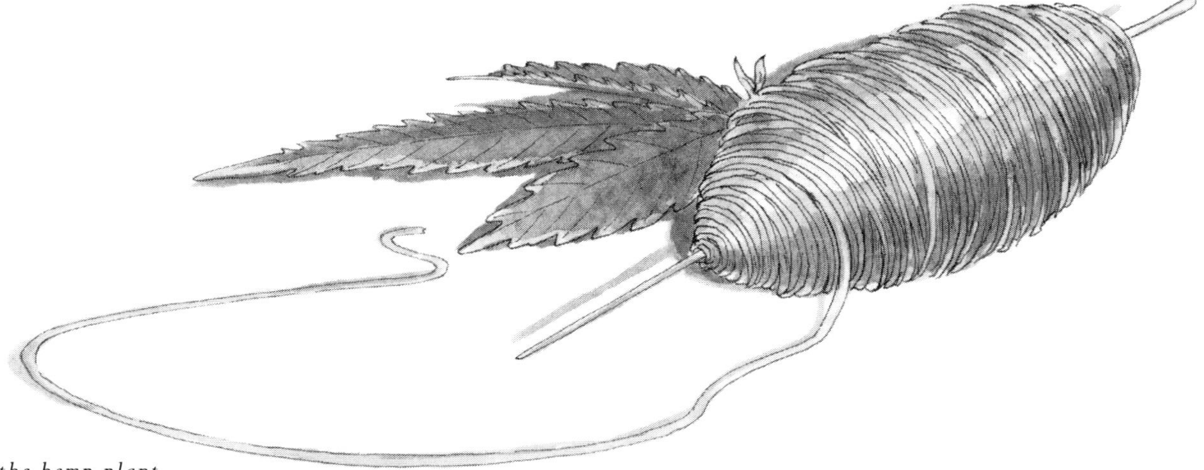

Threads made from the hemp plant

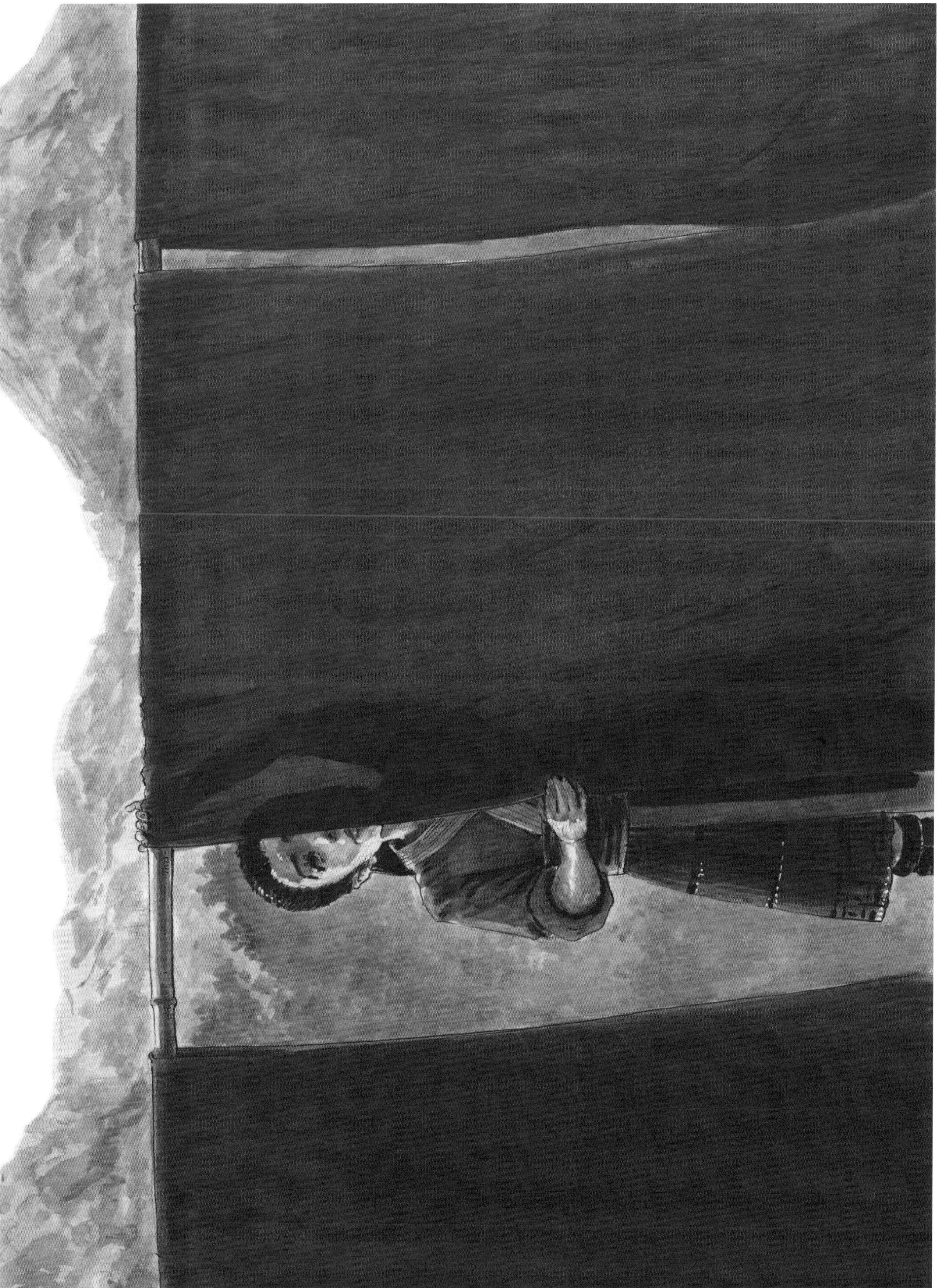

In a Patriarchal culture, women and girls are often doing menial work besides tending the fields and animals. Most girls have to get up before the sun and fetch water for cooking and cleaning, then go to the fields and work the garden and watch the children. Meanwhile, boys go to school or hunt and fish. Even if the girls were smarter than the boys, they were not allowed to go to school. The quick-witted girls hated the daily grind of work and chores and only dreamed of doing what most boys hate; to go to school. Life is not fair, and for those who have struggled against the norm, they have risen to achieve great success. They became nurses during the Vietnam War and translators for the doctors.

Now there are women in all facets of work that are not locked down by cultural practices. Coming to the United States allowed everyone to have equal dreams. What our parents and grandparents suffered opened the doors to enrich our lives. As each one of us strives to reach our dream, remember to lift the ones who gave up theirs so you may have your chance.

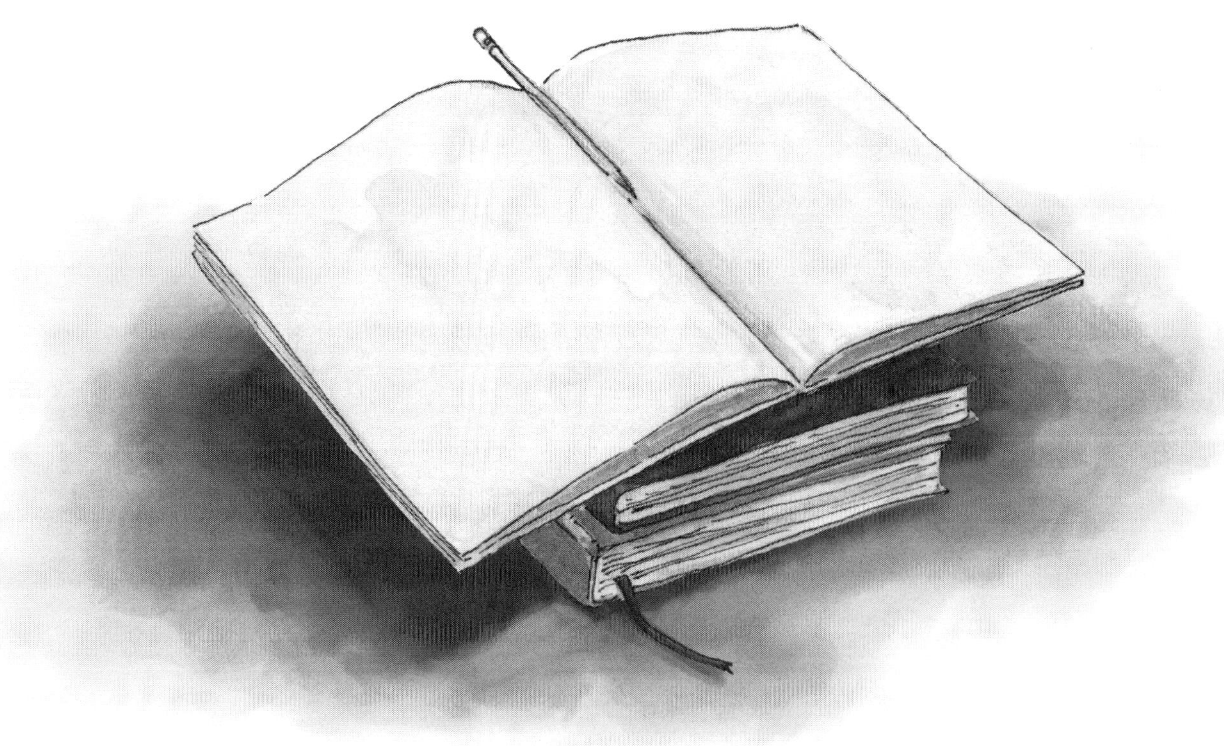

New books for a new life

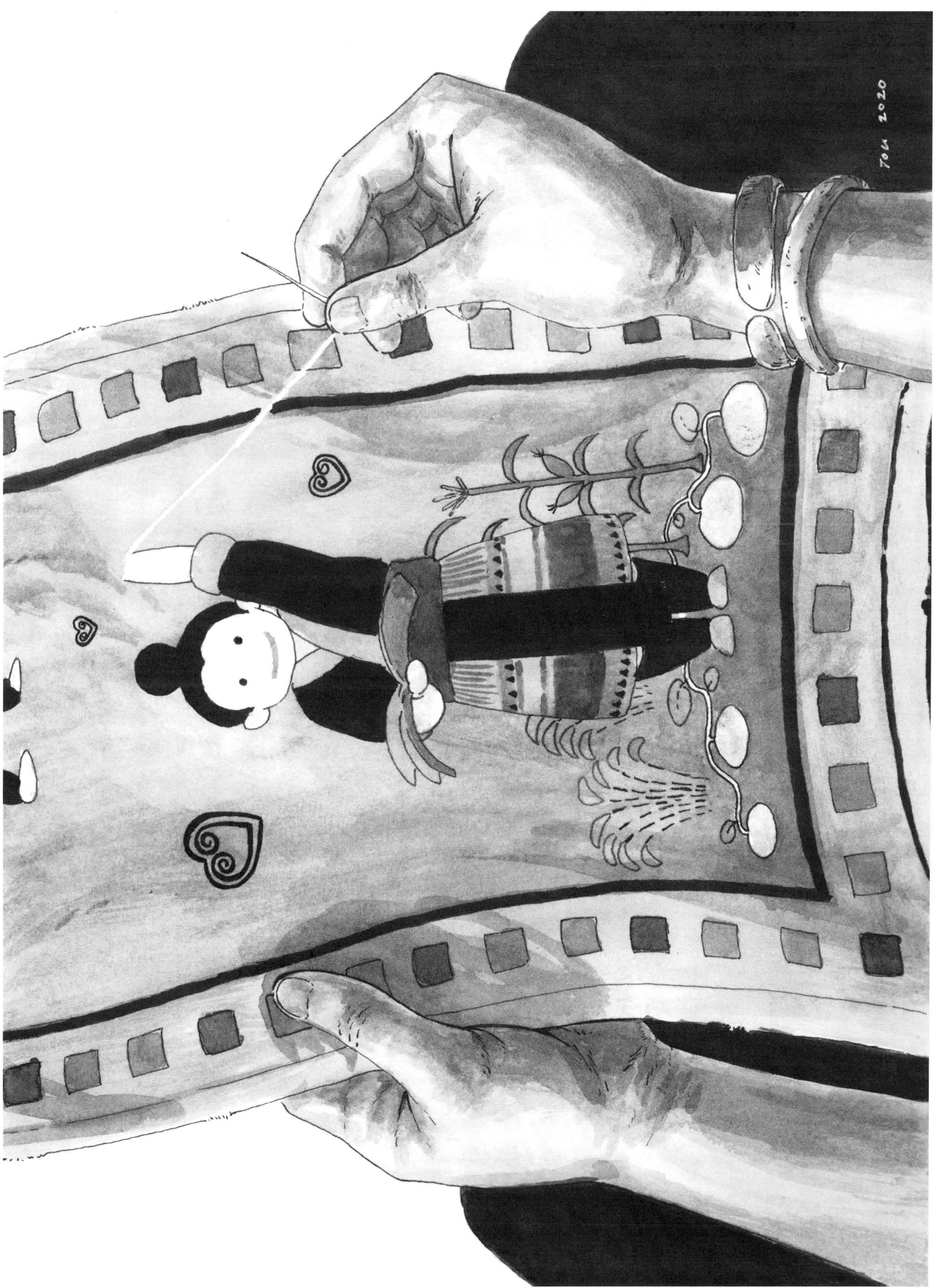

Black

During traditional weddings, a black umbrella plays an essential role in the ceremony. The groom's side must provide a long black umbrella with a hooked handle. There must also be a siv ceeb tied around the umbrella. A siv ceeb is a striped piece of cloth that represents a woman and is typically seen worn around single girls' purple headdress. The umbrella is like a ward to protect the bride and groom from bad luck during the wedding. Many things can happen from the trip to her parents' home and back to his family home, especially when they had to traverse mountains and valleys.

After the traditional wedding is complete and the newlyweds are home, the umbrella must be placed opened inside the newlywed's bedroom for three days so their marriage will be blessed.

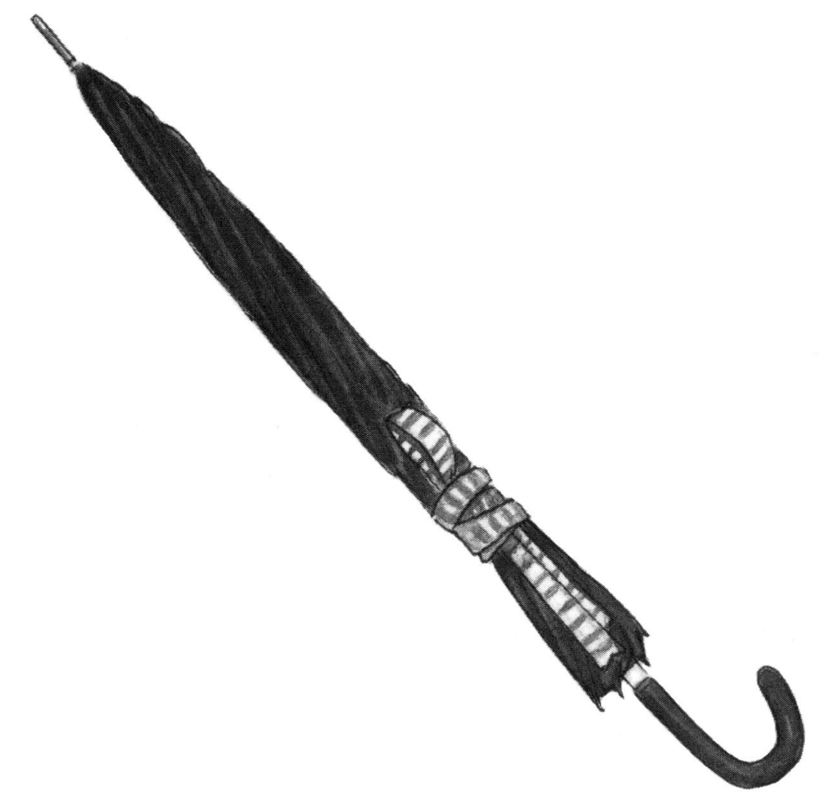

An wedding umbrella with a siv ceeb

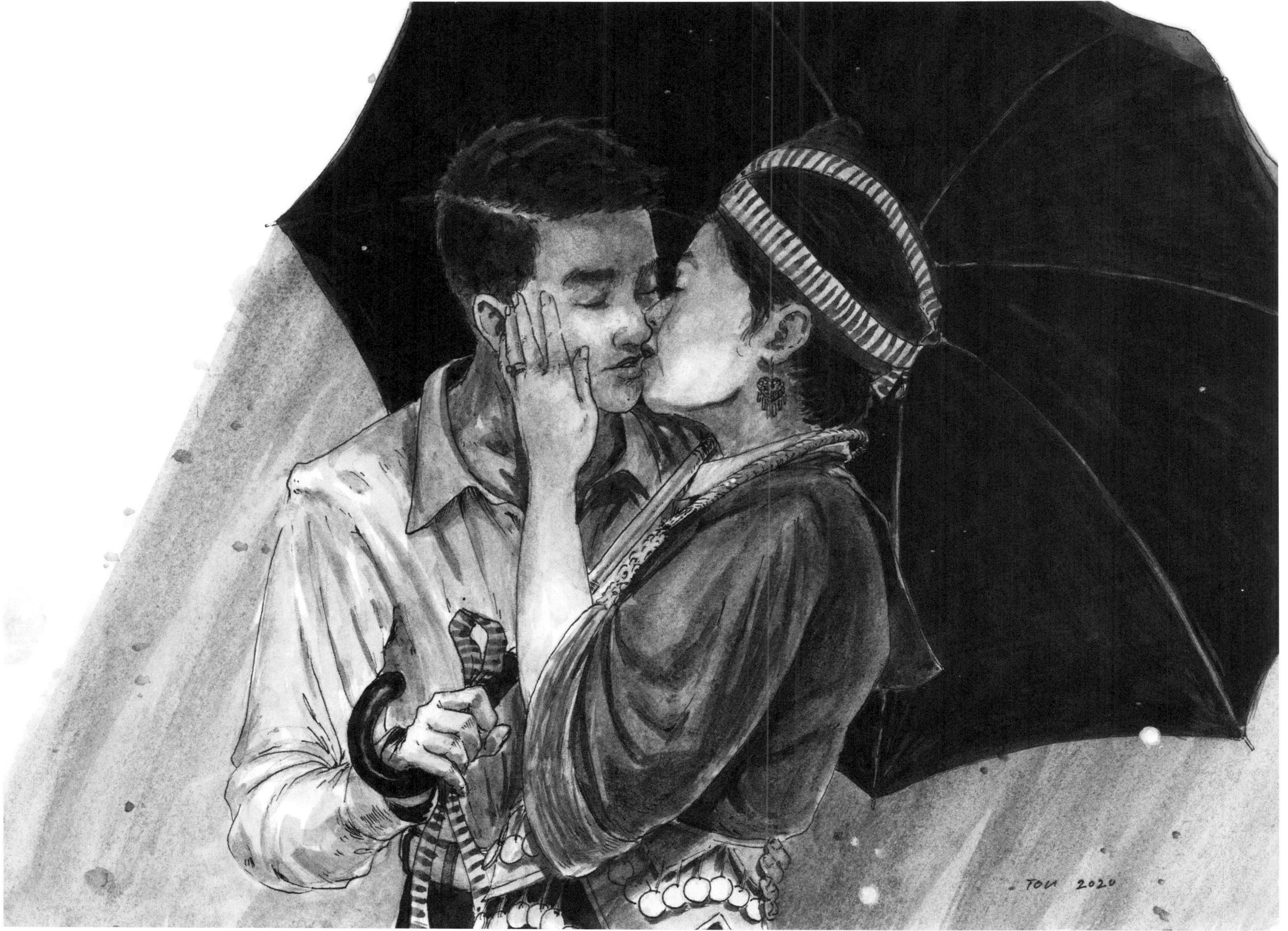
TOU 2020

Silver

After the Chinese beat the Hmong, they began to destroy their identity. They started by destroying the knowledge of the Hmong written language and then enslaving the survivors. To set them apart from others, the Chinese made these necklaces that they were forced to wear, called a Xauv. In Hmong, xauv means to lock.

Through the years, the Hmong have transformed these necklaces into a work of art. Intricate strings of interlocking silver rings are handcrafted to show prosperity and prestige. Xauv's are usually worn by boys and girls to the New Year celebrations to show off and attract a suitable mate. A xauv is gifted with a set of Hmong clothes to the daughters at their wedding as a dowry for her new life.

Many families have xauv's that have been passed down for many generations. The Secret War caused many of these heirlooms to be lost during the exodus and massacres. It is harder now to find an authentic silver Xauv. Knowledge of how to make one is becoming a lost art as the older generation no longer makes any. Finding an authentic one today costs hundreds, if not thousands of dollars. If you have one, know that you are loved and appreciate the history that you have been given and share the story with your children.

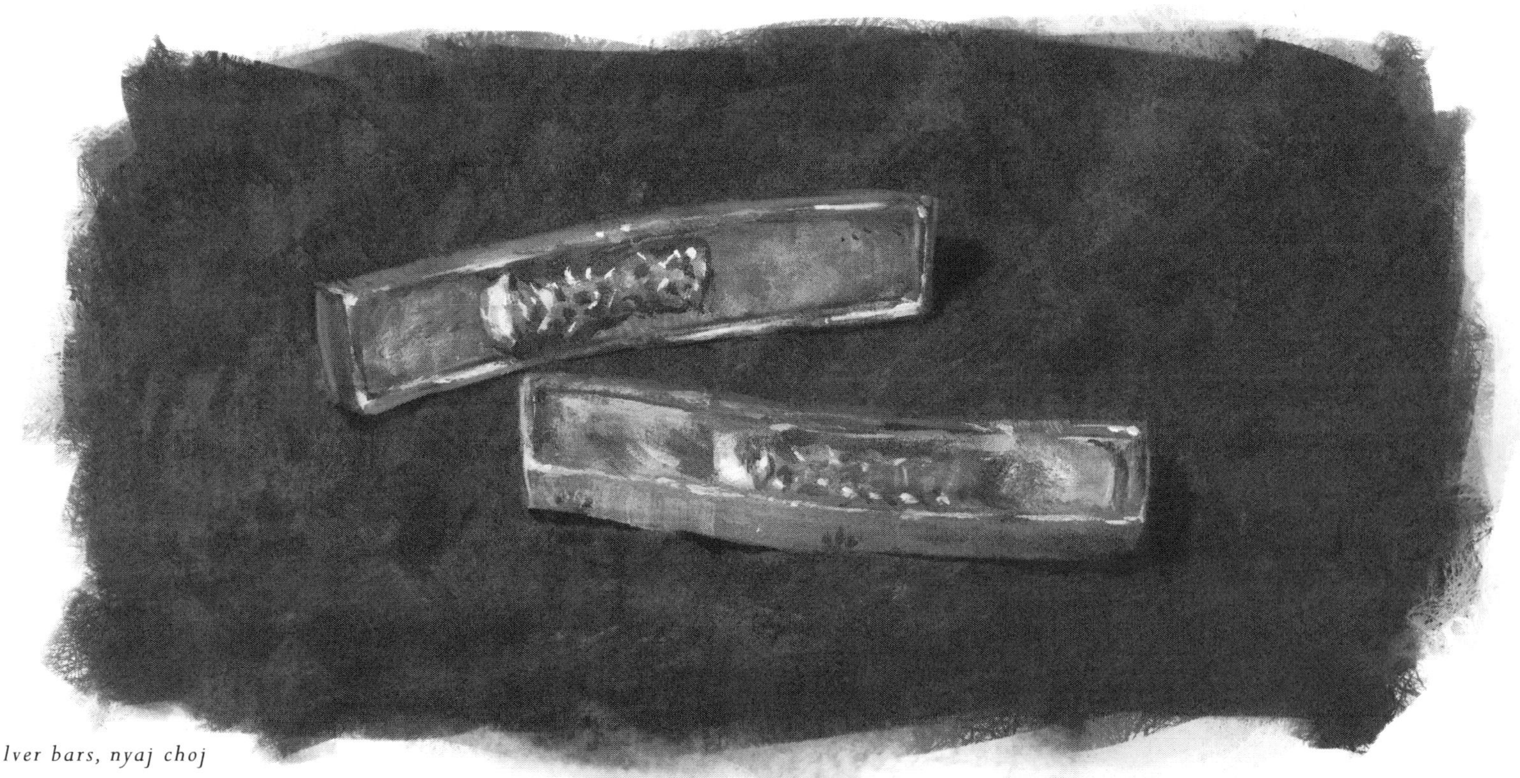

Silver bars, nyaj choj

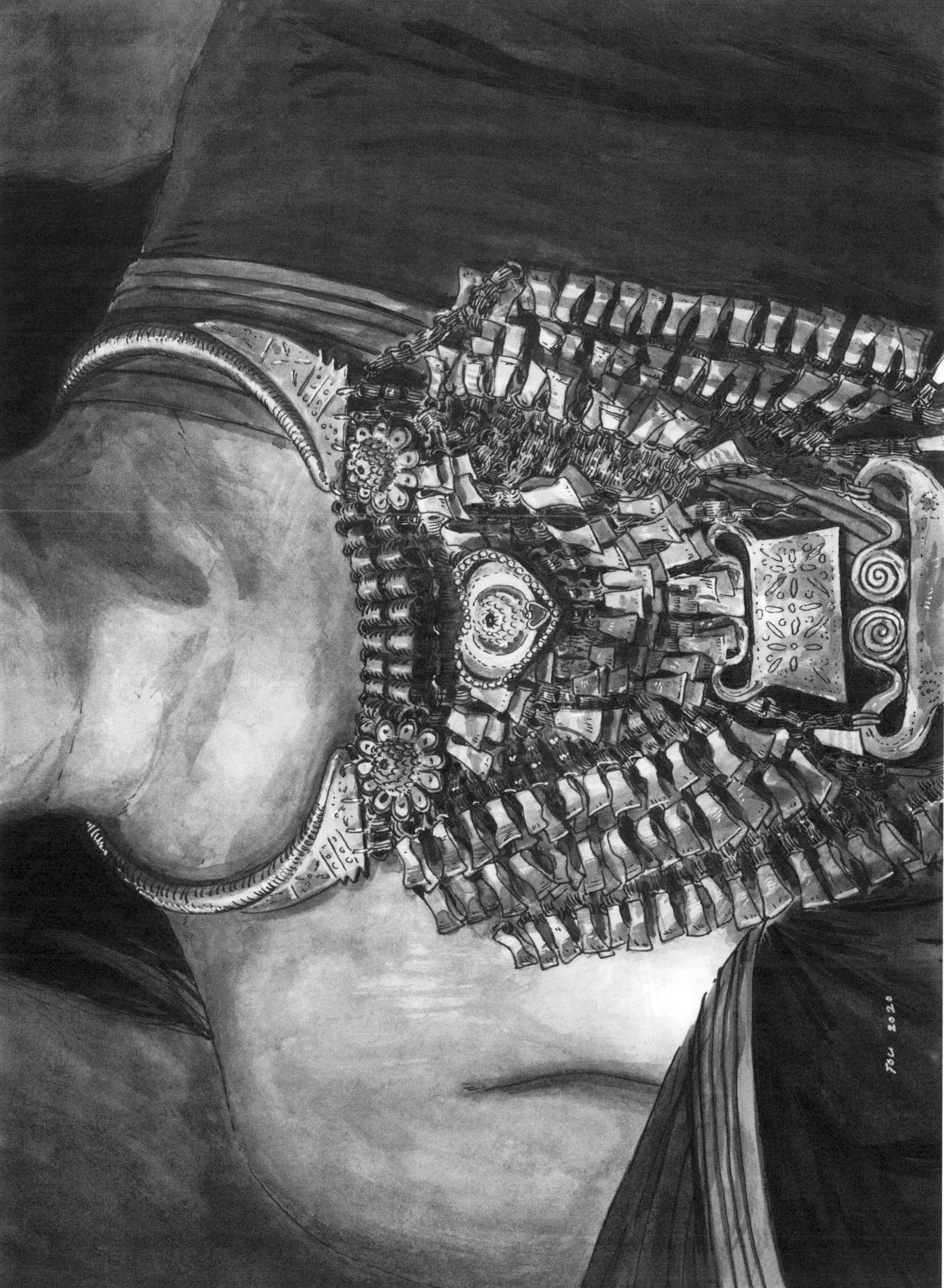

The Hmong skirt is a thing of beauty to behold. An original is hand-stitched with different patterns and then hand-pleated to maintain the distinct folds. A skirt may take over a year to make, and after each wearing must be re-pleated to hold the folds. There is so much labor that goes into these skirts, all the dreams of the maker are distilled in these threads. If you have one, count your blessings because they are not made like this anymore.

My mom told me that the original Hmong patterns were the Hmong language. It was hidden from the Chinese after all language and text by the Hmong were destroyed. To preserve the culture and teach it to the next generation, they sewed them onto their clothes. With time the patterns have lost meaning and have been simplified or altered so much that it has become just decorative. There is so much beauty and sadness when you look at what we have lost through the diaspora.

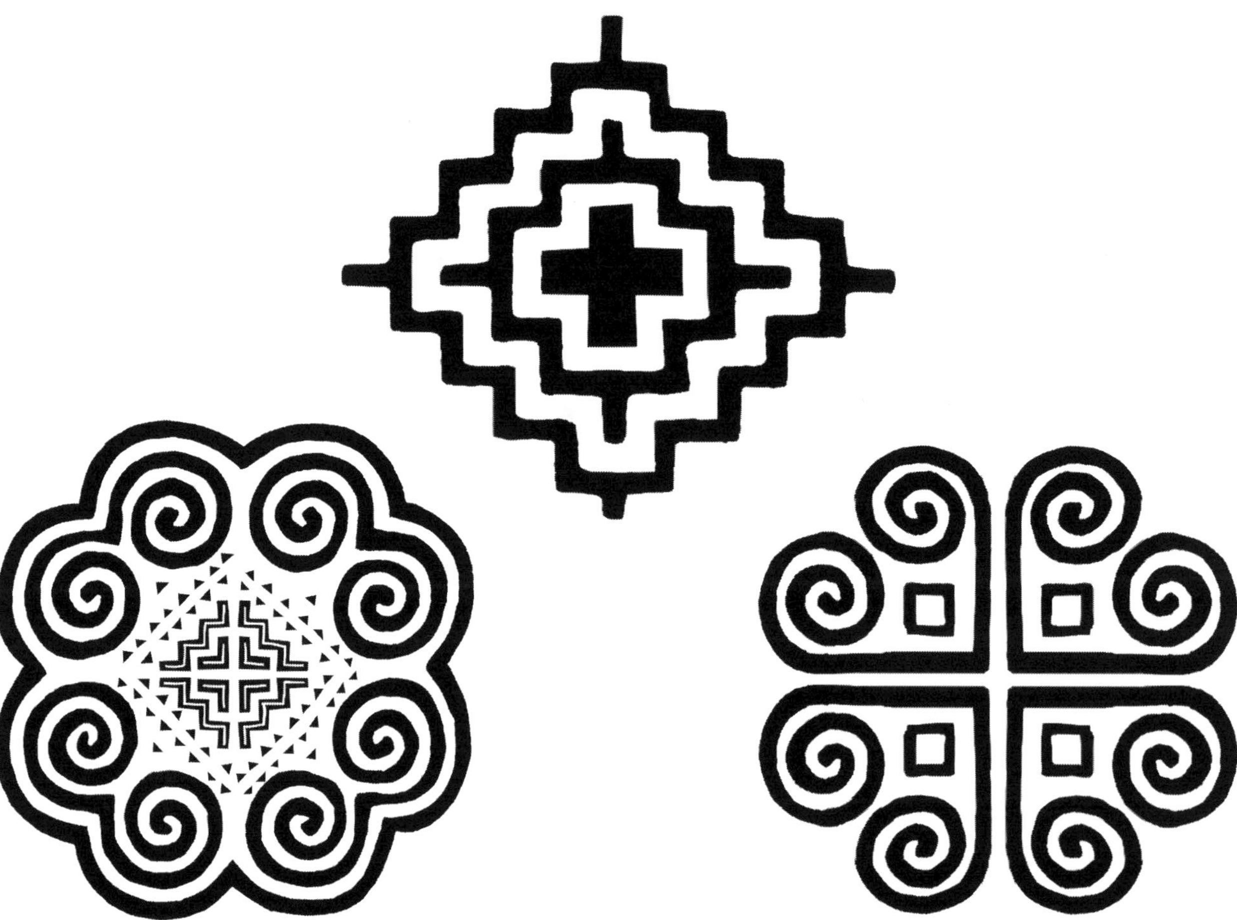

Traditional paj ntaub patterns

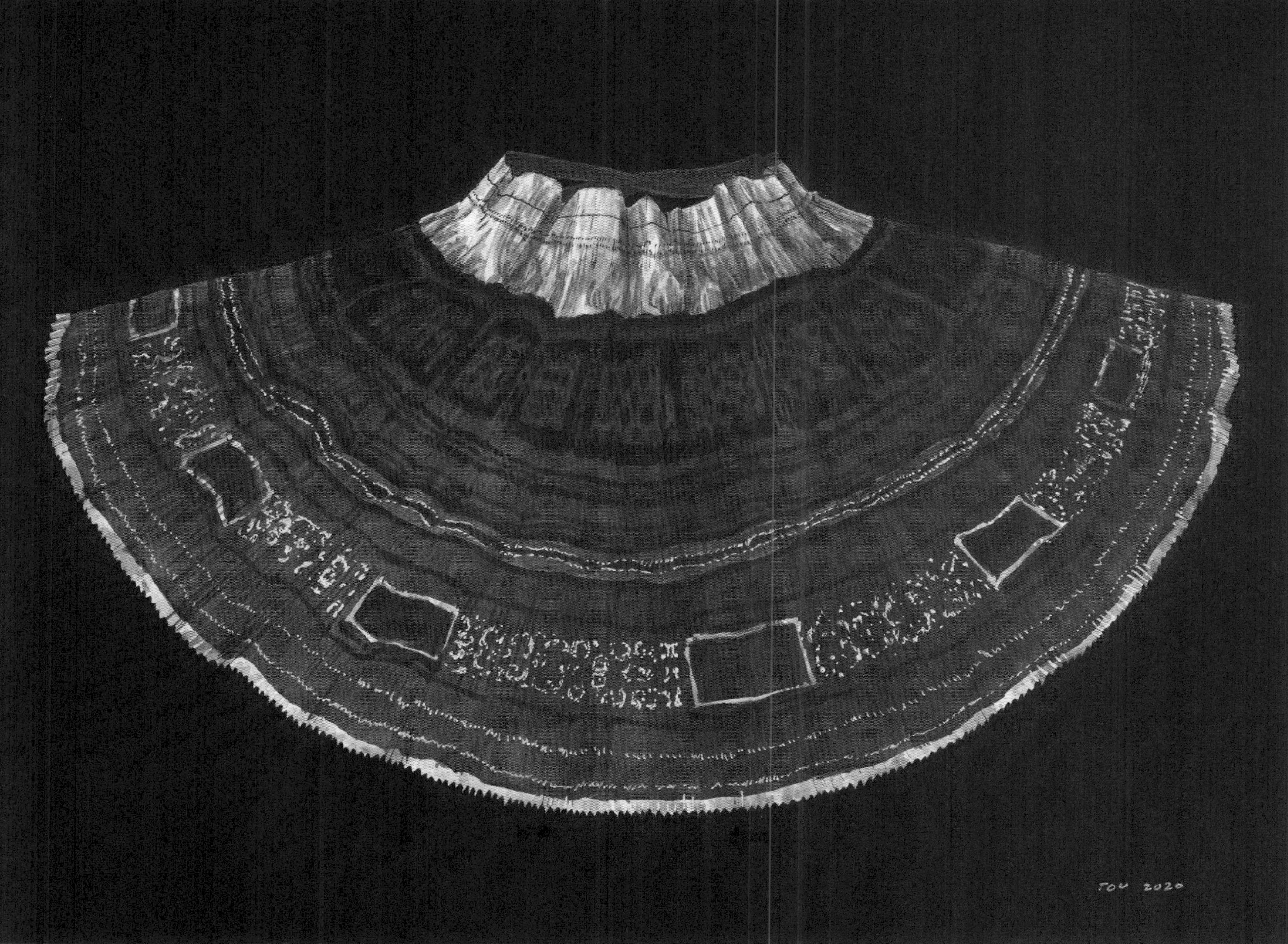
TOU 2020

Hunt

Pre-Vietnam War, the Hmong people, had access to firearms through the French Indochina War. They were mainly supplied by the French colonists and passed down from father to son. Many families used the Montagnard style musket rifles for hunting with, and when the Secret War began, they used them in battle.

My grandfather, Xai Dang, was said to be an excellent hunter and marksman. He provided food for the family and bartered some away for other necessities. His time as a hunter was cut short with an injury to his leg when he stepped on a buried mine during the Secret War. Buried mines were one of the many dangers hunters faced in the mountains of Laos.

Among these mines are the remaining 80 million bombs, from the 270 million dropped during the Secret War, that never detonated. Today they lie in the mountains and valleys undetected and active. Some have taken the lives of men, women, and children as they worked in the fields or walking to school. The effort to clean up the undetonated bombs continue to this day.

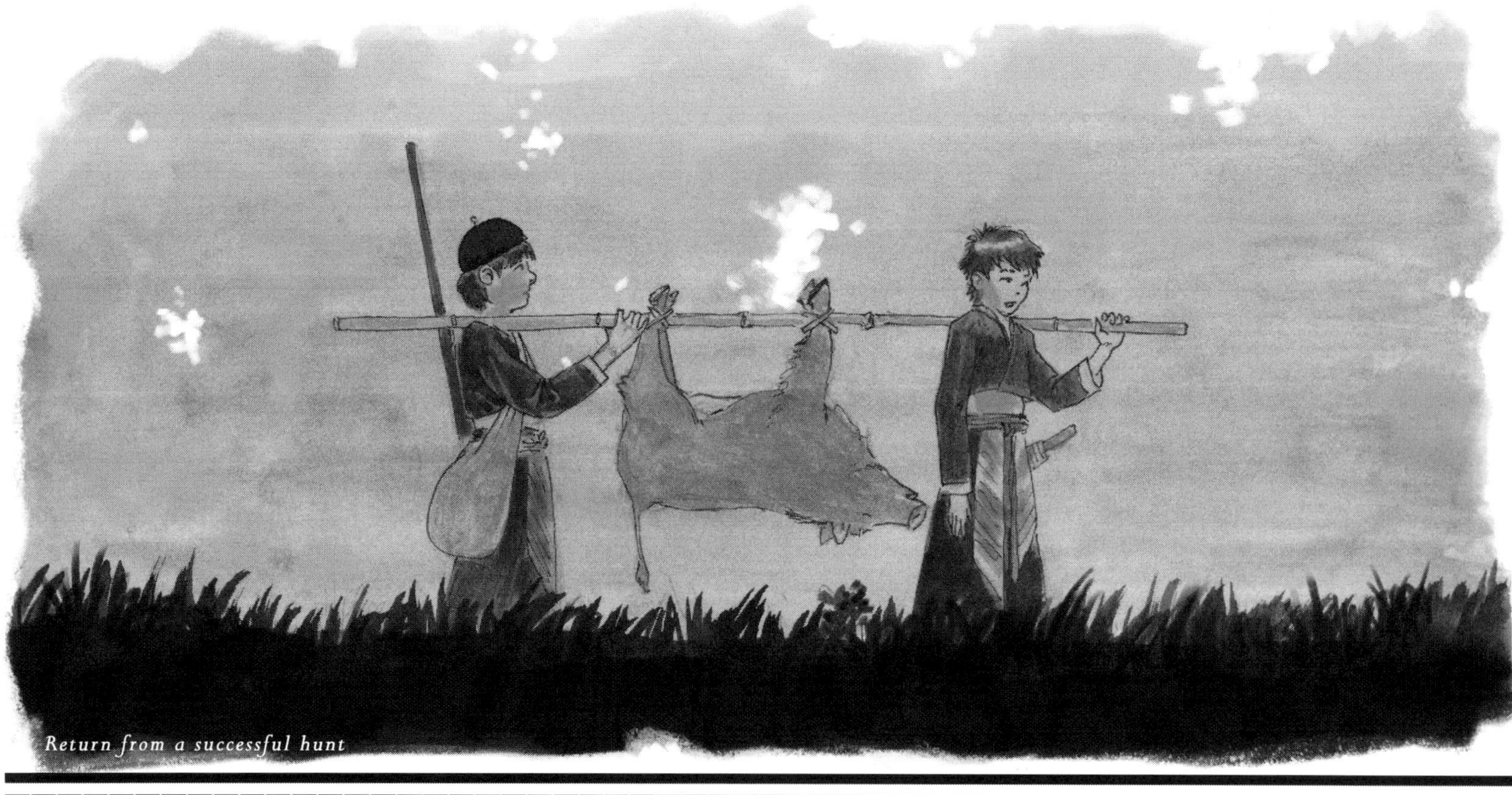

Return from a successful hunt

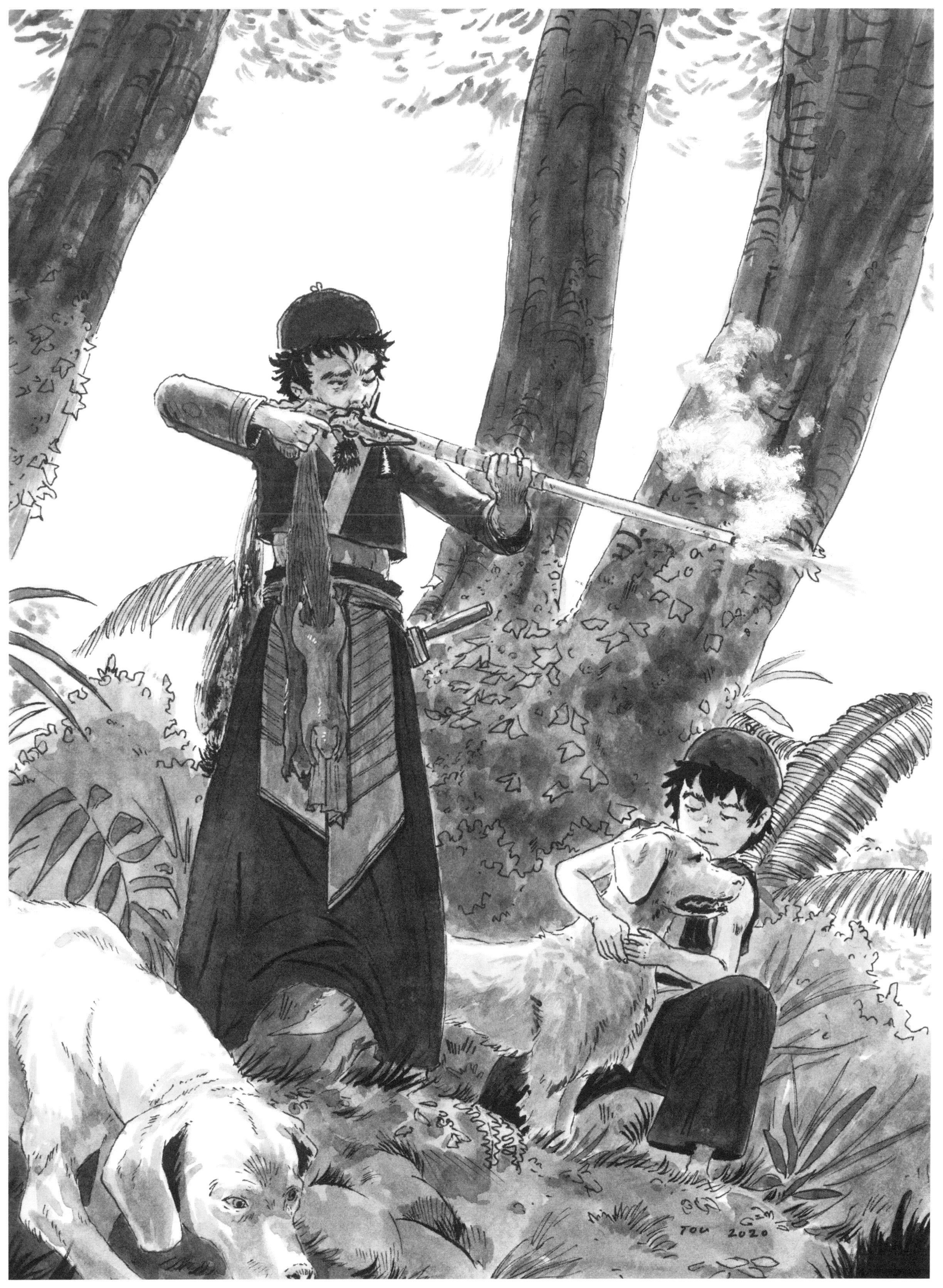
TOU 2020

Shaman

Animism is a practice that many Hmong families follow. It is a belief in the spirit world and that all things are connected through spirits. A spiritual leader is called a Shaman, who can communicate and interact with the spirit world. Animists believe the ancestral spirits are guides and protectors of the family.

When a family is stricken with an illness that physical medicine cannot cure they call a Shaman to come and access if it is a spiritual illness. If the Shaman determines it is, the family must provide an offering and sacrificial burnings to find the person's spirit.

The Shaman will enter the spirit world with chants and the sounds of drums and bells. They walk the spirit world to seek the fled spirit and help it find its way back to the person. Sometimes it is easy, but it is often dangerous because human spirits are not the only thing in the spirit world.

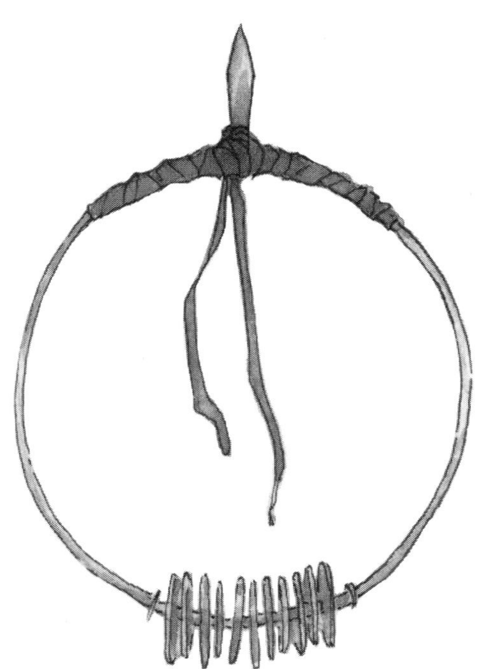

A tool for shamans to communicate with spirits

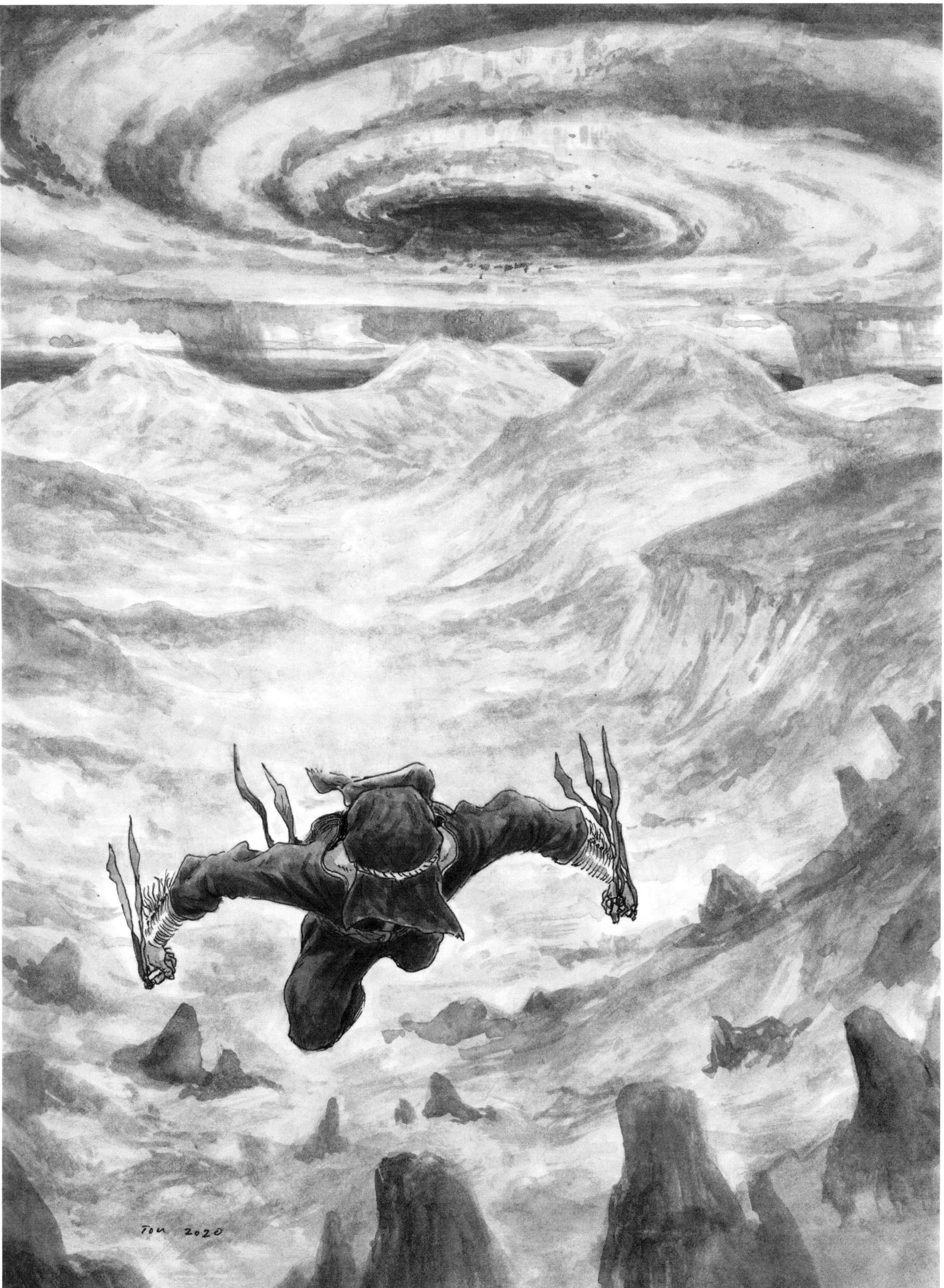
TOU 2020

Qeej

A Qeej is an instrument made of bamboo and reed. It is referred to as a mouth organ because of the sound it makes. There are a variety of similar instruments scattered throughout South East Asia. But what makes the Hmong Qeej different is that it is not used as just a musical instrument. It is a way to speak to the deceased. If you know what to listen for, each note has a meaning that can be translated into Hmong. The Hmong language is tonal and has 8-octave ranges. A Hmong word may have up to 8 different intonations that give the word a different meaning.

A Txiv Qeej, the lead qeej player, has to play special songs for the dead to awaken the humans' three main spirits and set them on the path to the next life. The first spirit stays with the body and becomes an ancestral spirit. The second spirit goes into rebirth, hopefully into the same family. Lastly, the third spirit returns to the spirit world and wanders there. These paths are said to be made when the proper songs are played on the Qeej, directing and showing the spirits the way. If they are not played properly, the spirits will become restless.

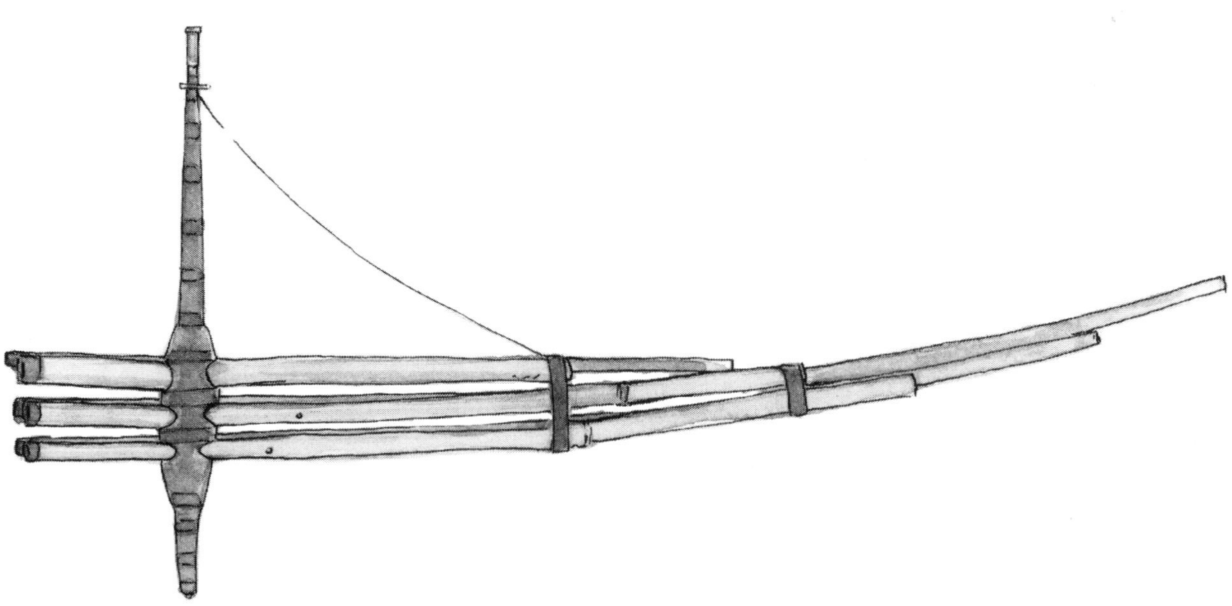

Traditional Hmong qeej

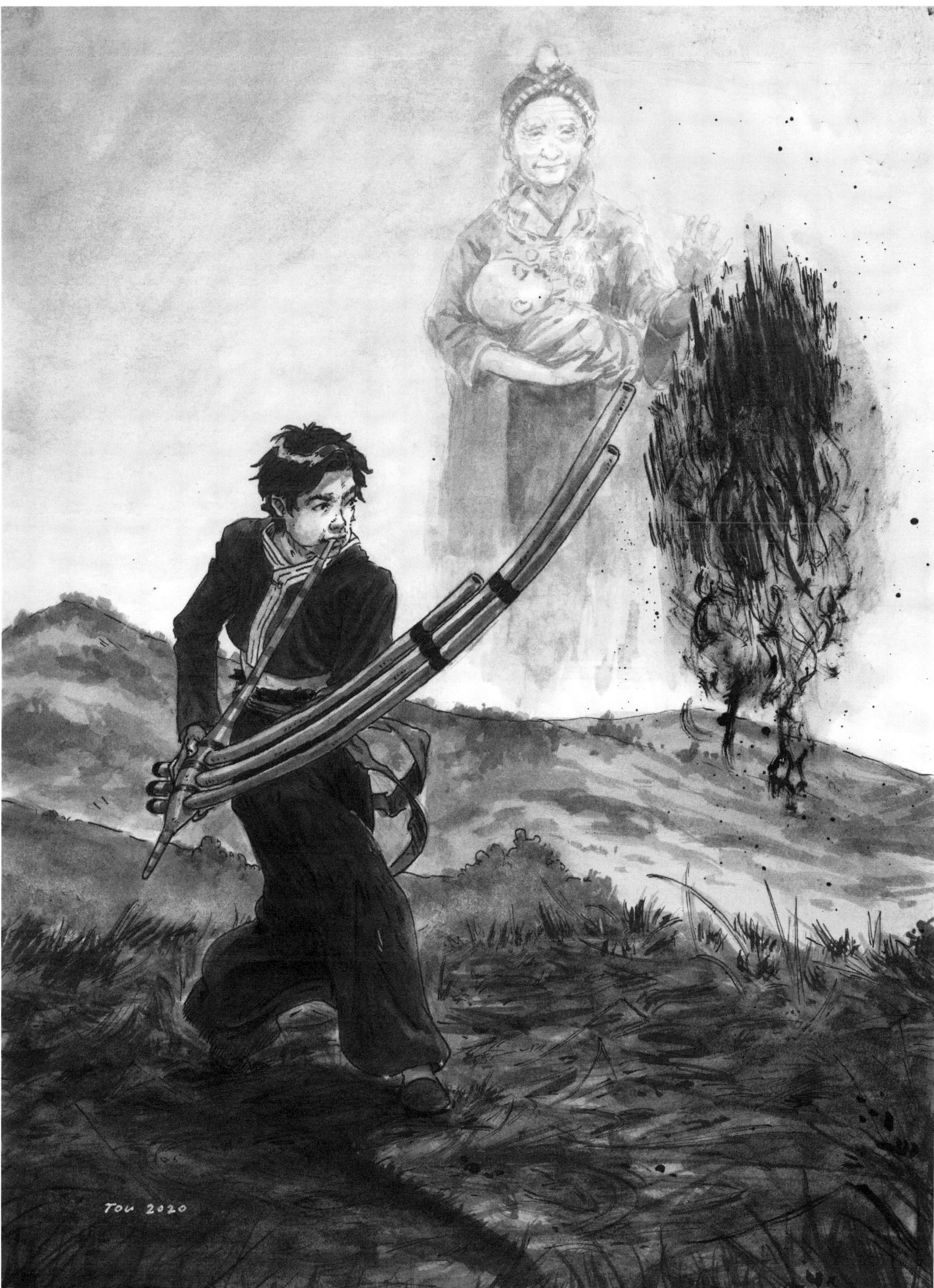
TOU 2020

String

In 1947 under the directive of the Christian and Missionary Alliance, C&MA, Reverend Ted Adrianoff, and his wife were sent to Xieng Khouang, Laos. They were tasked to bring the gospel to the people there. With the help of a local named Nai Keng, they went to the village, and the headman set them up in a haunted house. Under the watchful eye of the village shaman Boua Ya Thao, he wanted to see if the Missionaries God was stronger than the spirits of the haunted house. During this time, Boua Ya's cousin Jou Sang came home to visit his wife, who was living in Boua Ya's home. Jou Sang's wife had become deathly ill, and Boua Ya could not heal her spirit.

Boua Ya told Jou Sang about the white man and his God staying at the haunted house. Maybe their God could heal his wife? They went to the haunted house and asked Ted Adrianoff and Nai Keng to help heal Jou Sang's wife. Together, the two missionaries shared the gospel with the family, and after a while, the whole family converted to Christianity, including Boua Ya and Jou Sang. Miraculously Jou Sang's wife was also cured of her ailment and recovered. This first conversion snowballed into thousands more as Christianity spread among the Hmong.

During this time, my grandparents and parents came to Christ. They cut the strings of their old belief and put their faith in God to help and heal them. With their faith intact, they survived the exodus across Laos and the killings that took place after the Secret War. With the help of Christian churches in the Mid-West, many Hmong people were sponsored to the US. My family ended up in Wausau, Wisconsin, and grew up going to church and learning about God. The Hmong planted a church in Wausau called the First Hmong Missionary Alliance Church and have worked tirelessly to better the community. Today I carry on the beliefs of my parents and lead my family in trusting the Lord.

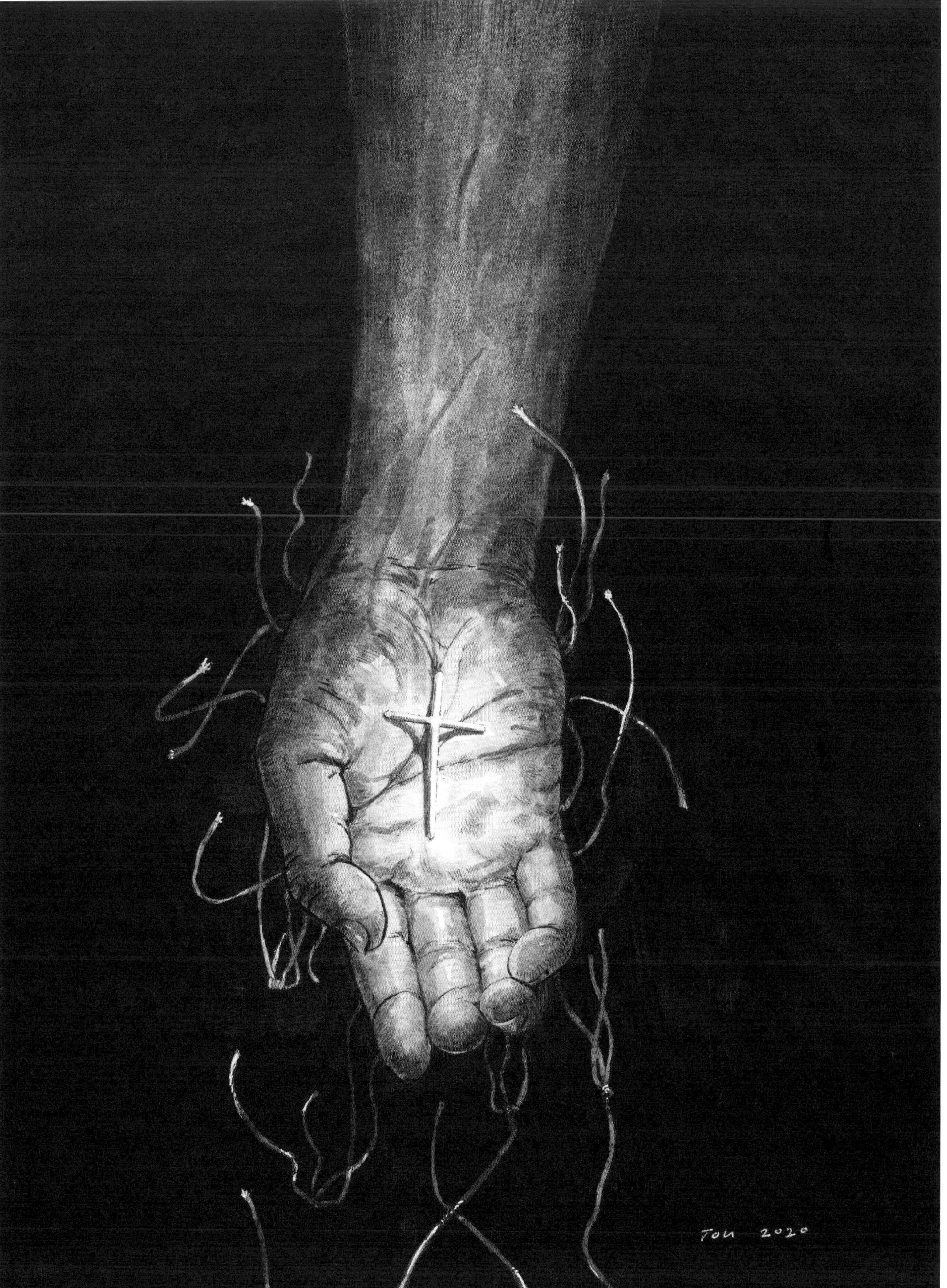
TOU 2020

Tool

As an agrarian community with low-level technology, a fire was the best tool for the Hmong to clear the land for farming. Families would help each other clear land with a controlled fire in exchange for labor. Although frowned upon by the modern world, the slash and burn technique had been used for hundreds of years in the mountains of South East Asia. No other way was faster than with fire.

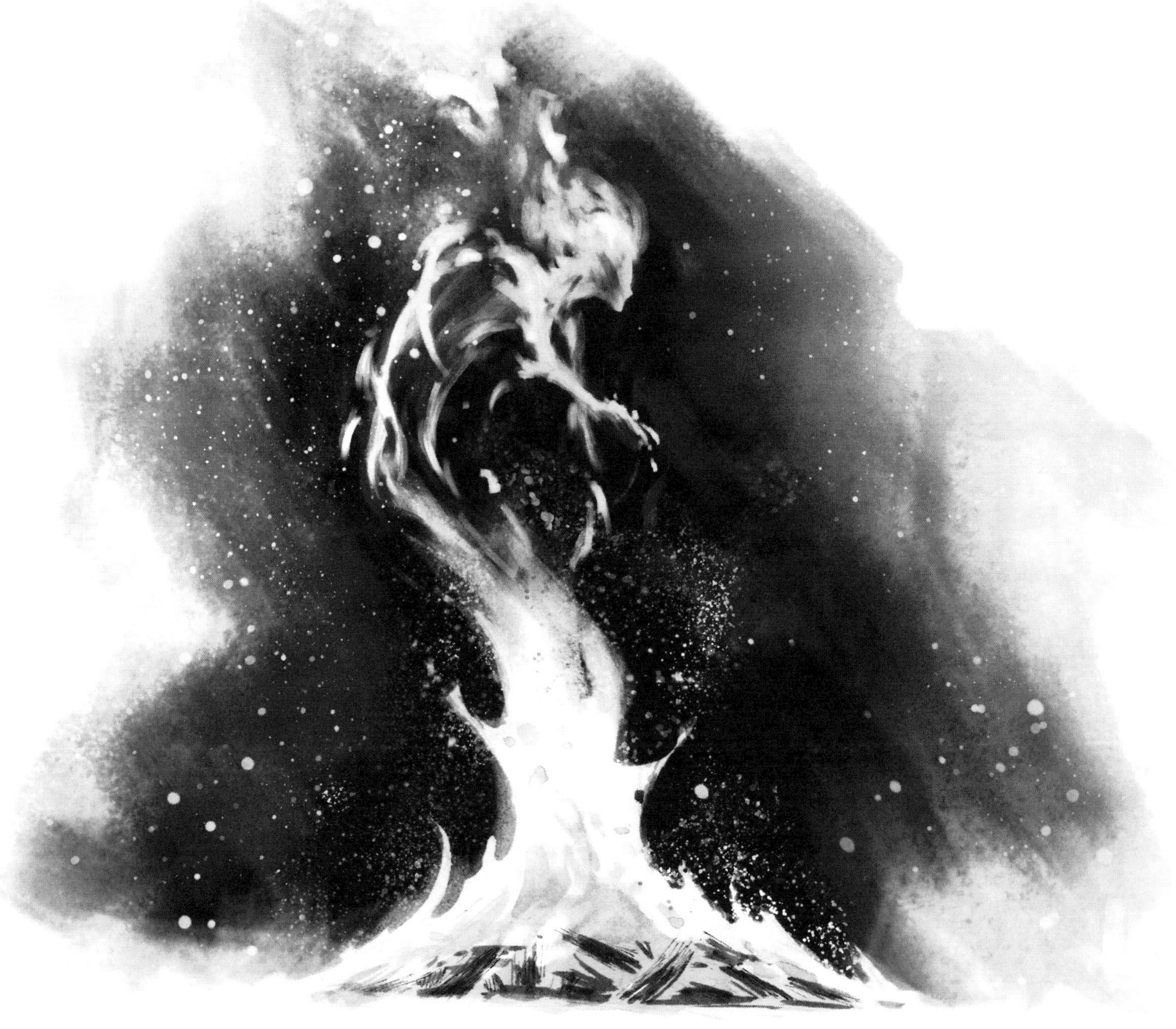

Fire elemental doing the bidding of man

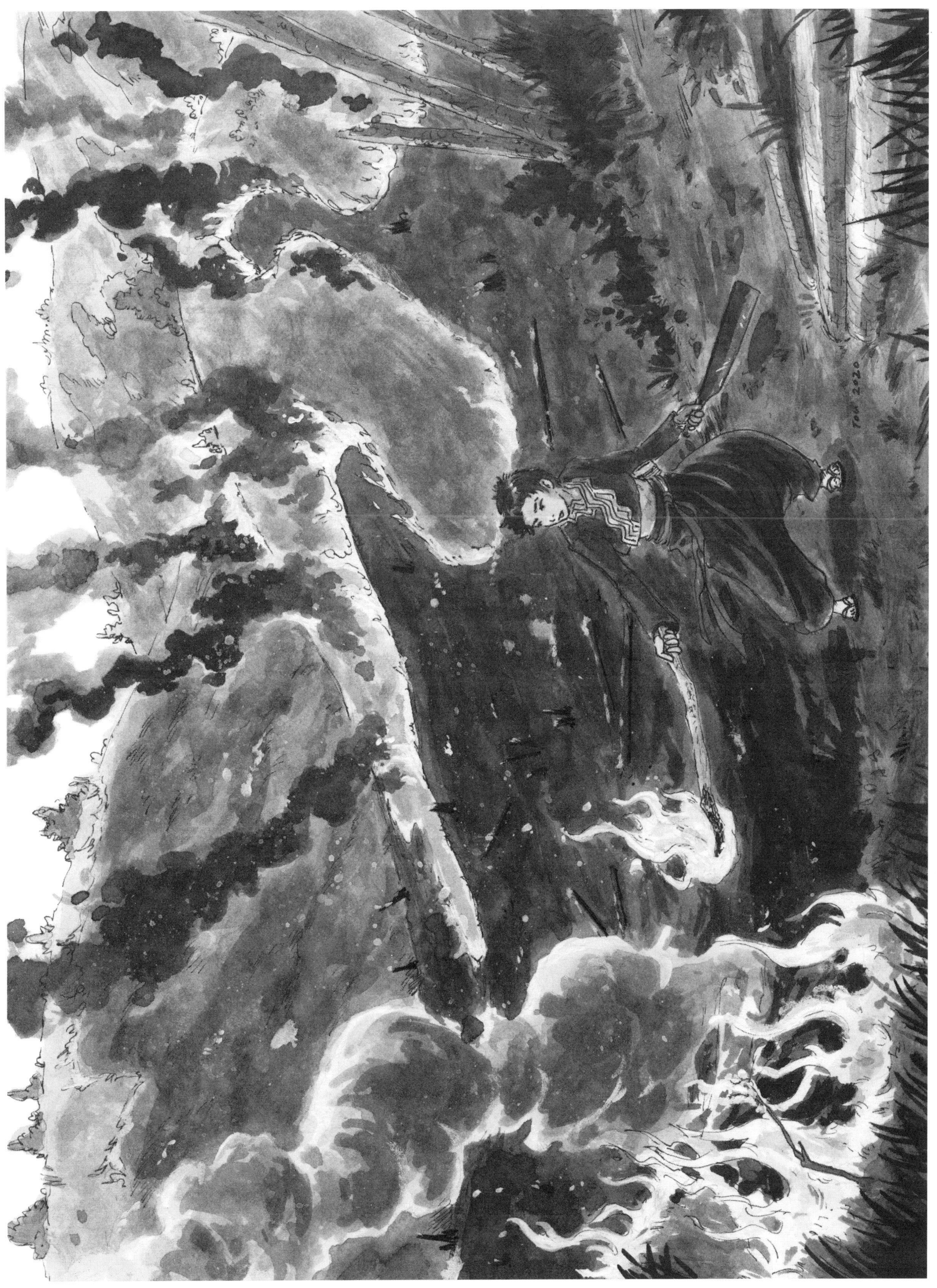

For thousands of years, the Hmong have grown rice. They were one of the first cultivators in China and had taught the skill to the Chinese. Each harvest, the hillside would be adorned with waves of gold. Each family worked tirelessly from sunup to midnight, trying to gather every last grain of rice. The rice would determine how well your family lived the next year. It was more precious than gold in remote mountainous villages.

After the rice stalks were bundled and collected, they were threshed to separate the grains from the stalk. Using a bamboo tray, called a vab, they gathered the rice grains and tossed the rice into the air to get rid of the inedible husk. With rice, they can make rice cake, porridge, noodles, and flour. It is the main staple of the Hmong's diet.

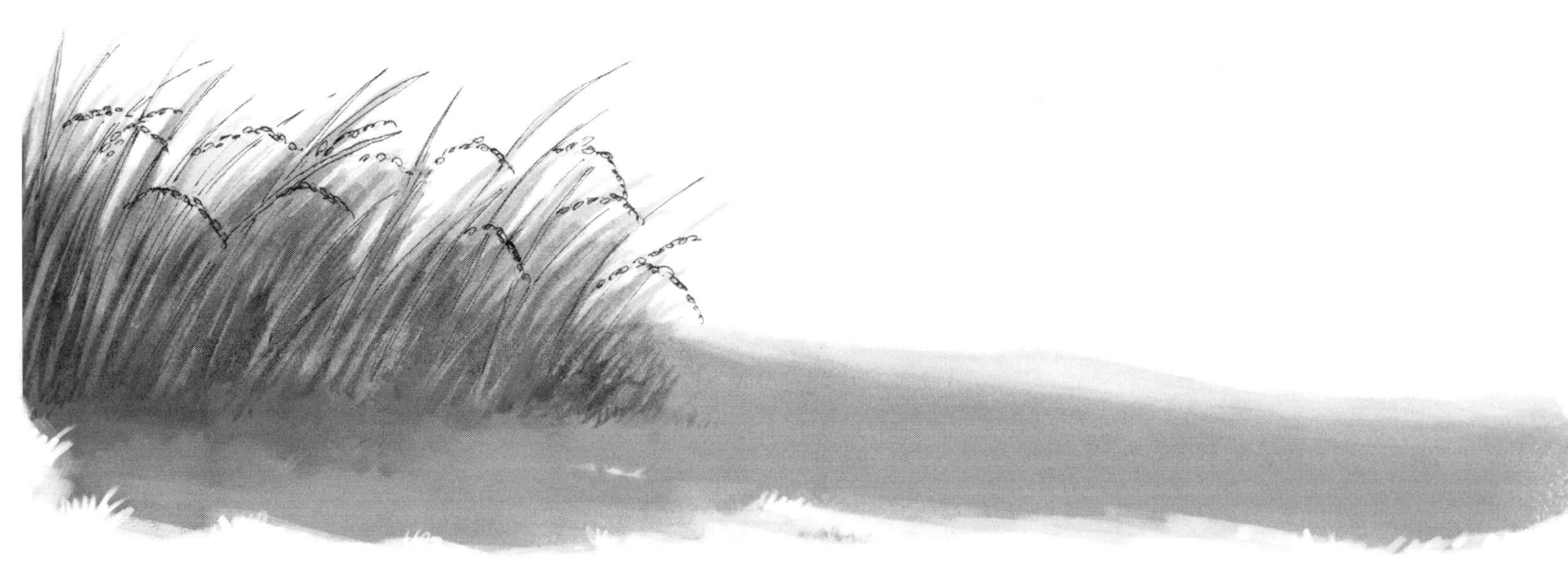

Rice field at harvest

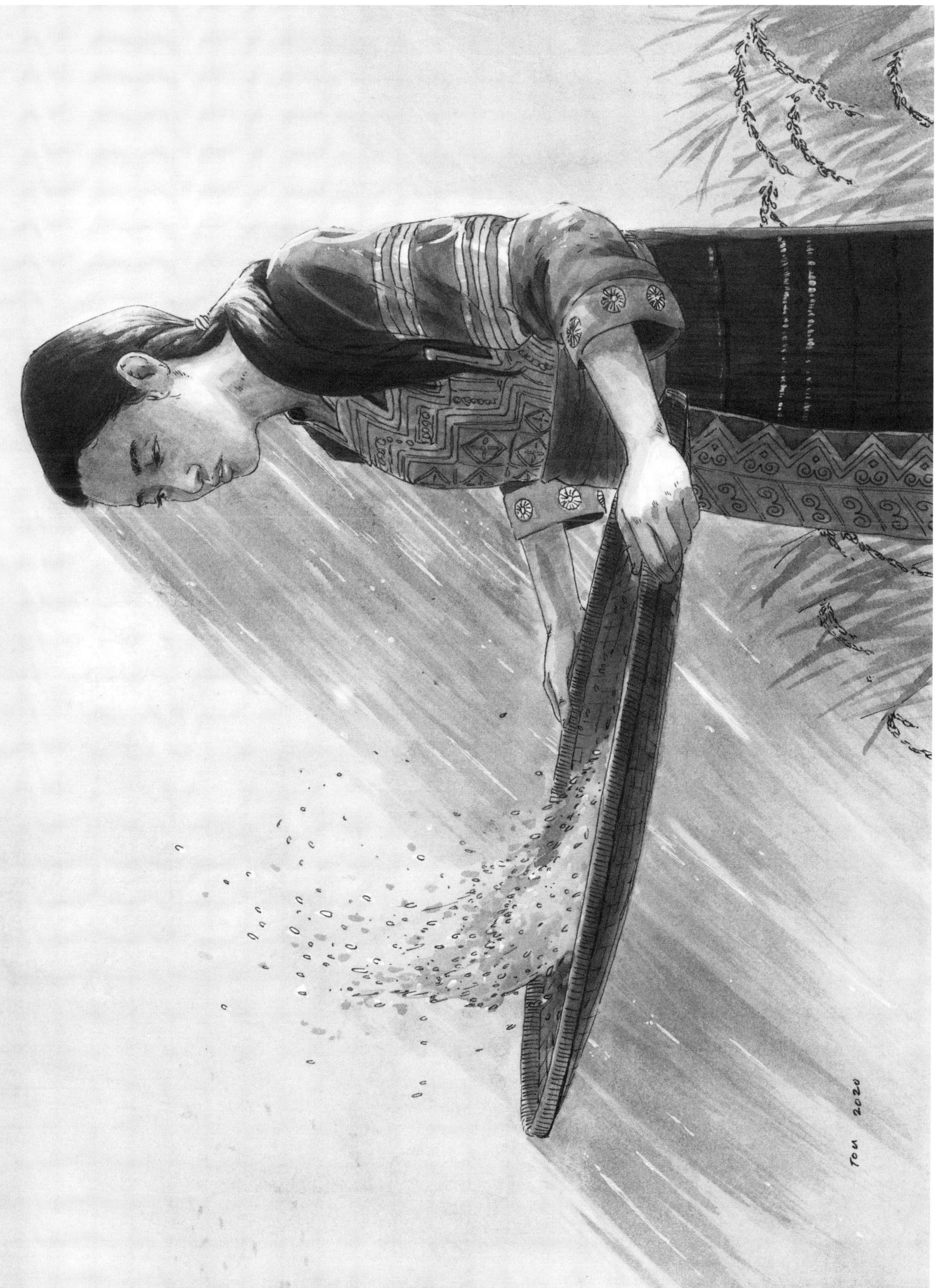

The Mekong River is 2703 miles long and sets the border between Laos and Thailand. It presented a major obstacle for the Hmong who fled the Pathet Lao for the refugee camps in Thailand.

The many months running across mountains and valleys took its toll on the families. Malnourished and tired, they stared in trepidation at the moving river. With Pathet Lao patrols behind them and boats patrolling the river, it seemed hopeless. Those lucky enough to have trade items bought passage aboard boats. The strong ones swam across. The unlucky ones were shot on the riverbanks or in the river during the night crossings.

Women and children were most affected by the crossing. Those without any men to help them begged and pleaded with strangers to aid them. With no help coming, they grabbed anything that floated and waded in. They would do whatever it took to make it across,even sacrificing themselves if it meant survival for their children.

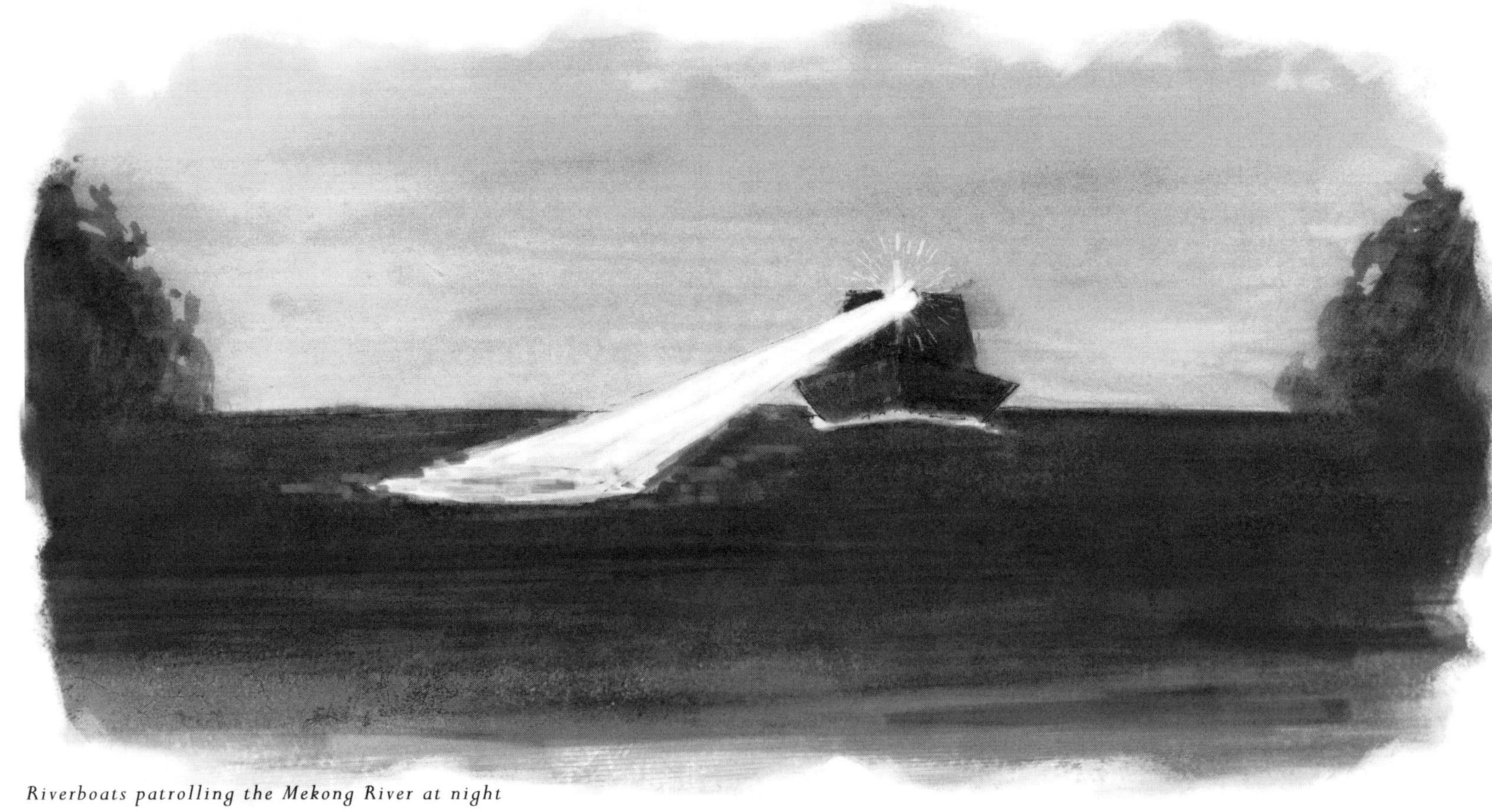

Riverboats patrolling the Mekong River at night

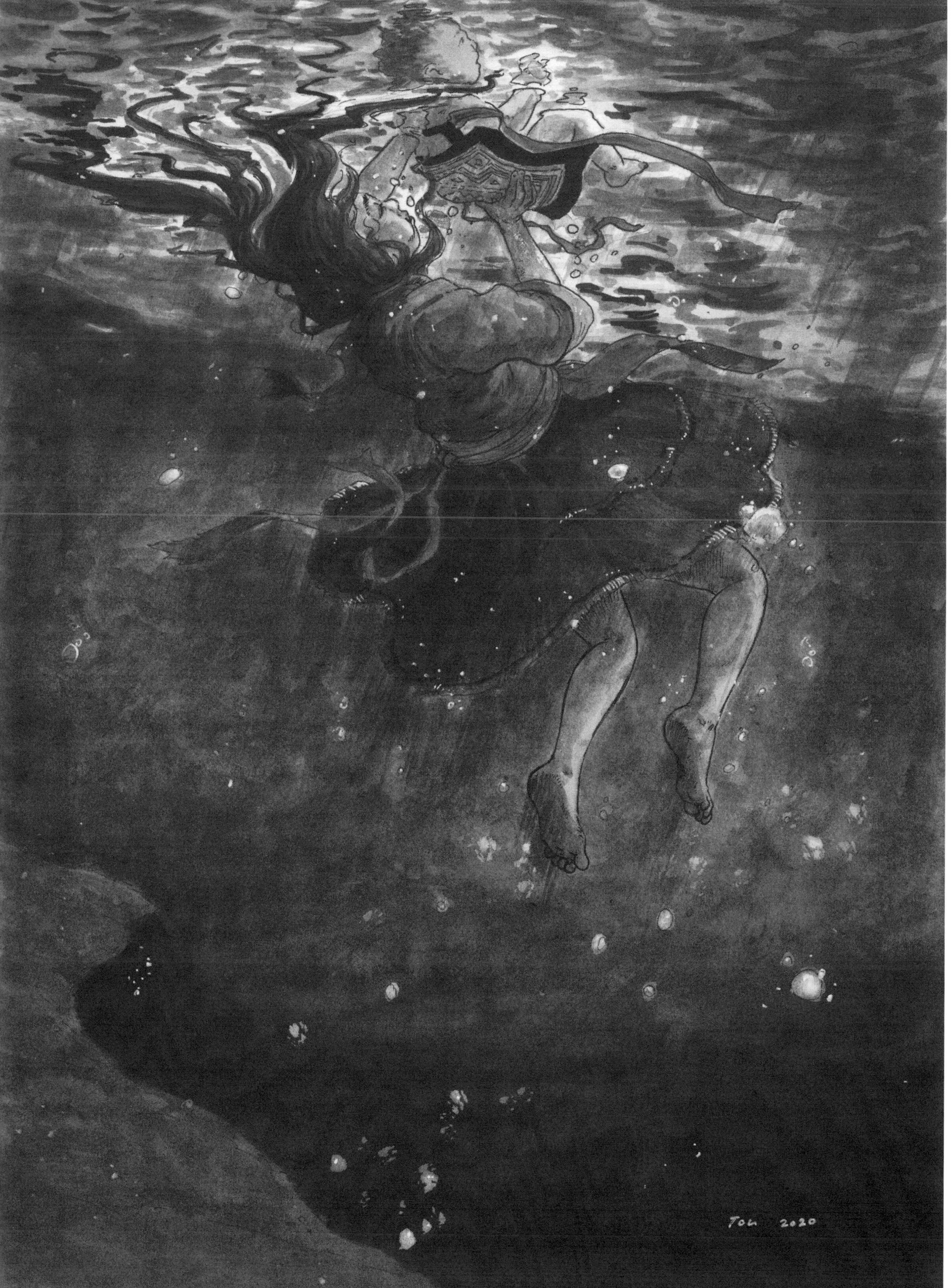
Tou 2020

Future

After the Secret War ended and General Vang Pao had fled Laos for the US. There was talk in Congress about bringing the Hmong refugees to the US for relocation. Congress's first thought was, "Yes, they helped us, so let us bring them here." But after finding out that the Hmong were mostly farmers with low education and living with low-level technology, there was a split leaning towards no. They doubted that the Hmong could contribute to American society and would just be a drain on the economy. It took the persuasive efforts of the CIA liaison and a Hmong soldier to convince Congress that the Hmong could adjust and contribute to America.

From 1975-1980, the first Hmong refugees were brought to America. Most of them ended up in the Midwest due to the American churches that sponsored the families. For the new residents, life in the US was hard for them to adjust to. From the snowy climate to learning a new language, finding work, raising children, and dealing with racism were the struggles, the first wave of refugees faced. It was an uncertain future but certainly better than dying in a Secret War.

After 40 years of being here in the US, the Hmong have proven their contribution to the US. There are Hmong doctors and lawyers, Senators and Mayors, small business owners, teachers, farmers, white- and blue-collar workers. They have done well in forty years. Imagine what their children may accomplish in the future.

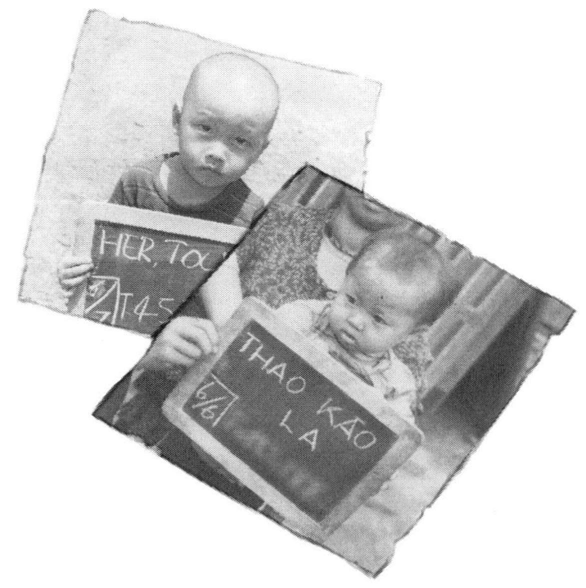

Pictures of my wife and I posing for our immigration photos.
We were both born in the refugee camp of Ban Vinai five years apart.

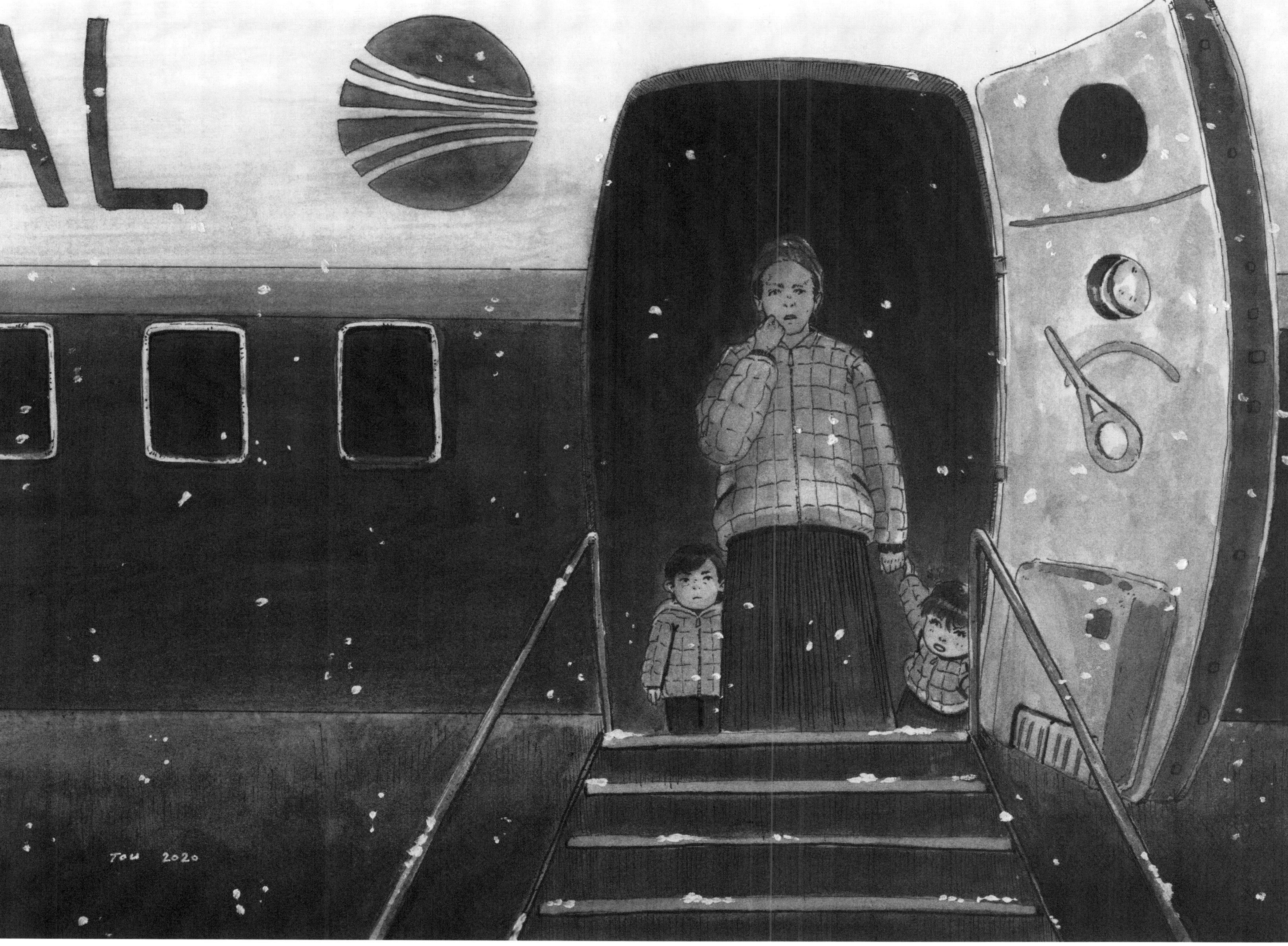
TOU 2020

There is no official memorial recognized by the government for the soldiers of the Secret War. My people were recruited by the CIA to fight the Vietnamese along the Ho Chi Minh trail. When all the men were recruited, and there were no more men to help the Americans, General Vang Pao ordered that anyone over the age of 11 had to help fight and bolster their forces. Many died before the war ended.

There is an unofficial memorial that exists in the US that commemorates the sacrifice of the secret allies. The Soldier Stone was built in 1995 and is in Colorado. The Hmong Veterans built another memorial in the city of Sheboygan, WI. There is a large Hmong population there due to the Hmong refugees' relocation after the Secret War.

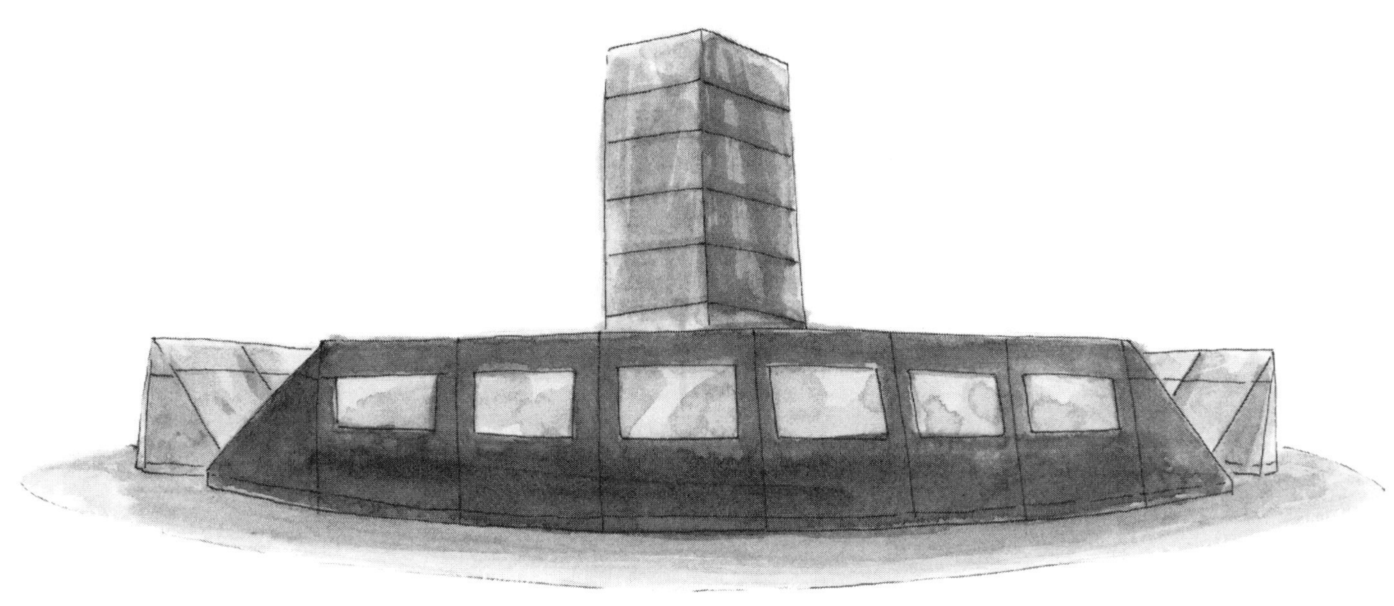

Artist representation of the Soldier Stone and Sheboygan Secret War Memorial

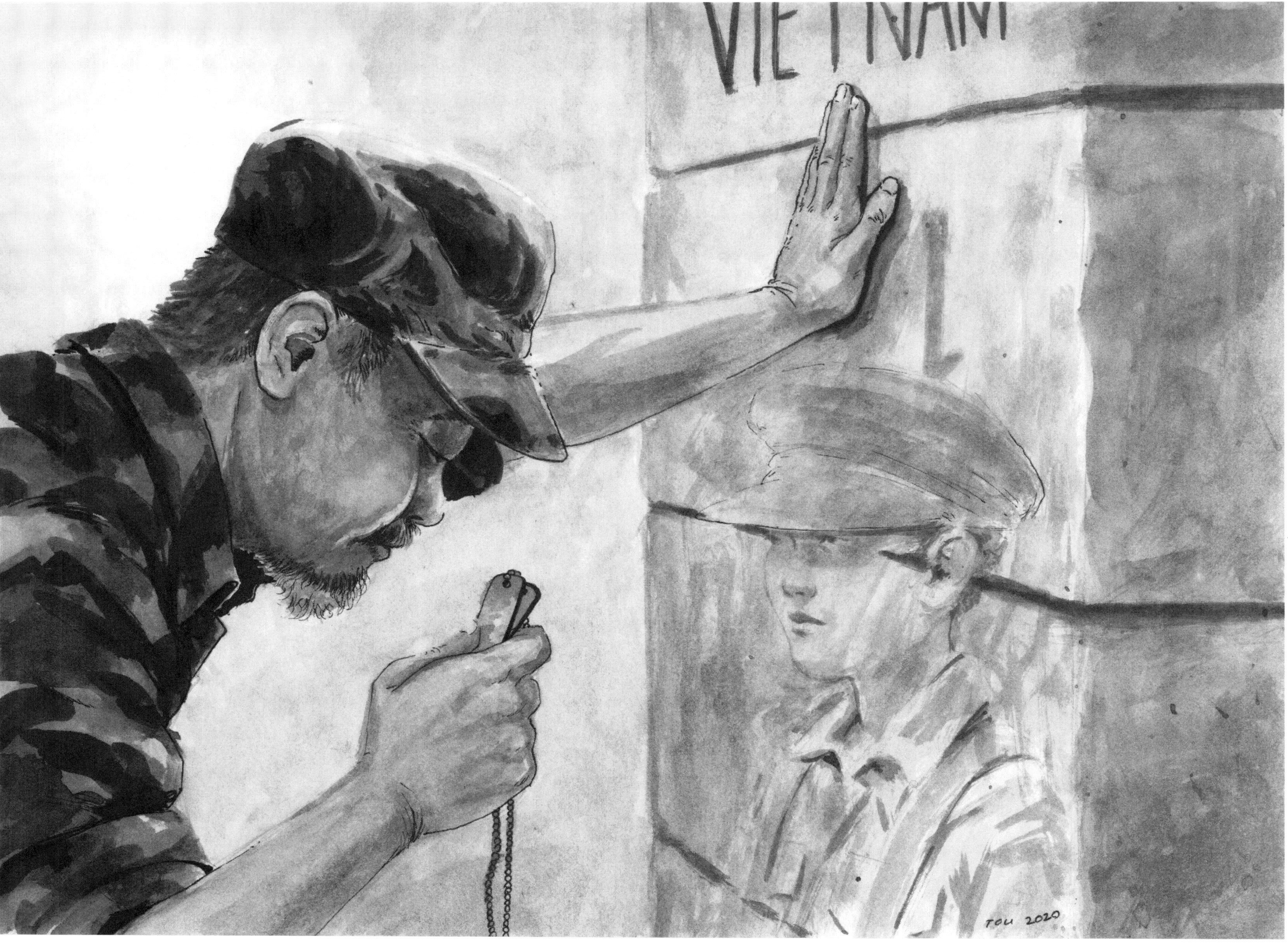
VIETNAM
TOU 2020

THANK YOU

Special thanks to the Facebook group, HManganime for organizing the prompts used for #hmongtober.

I am grateful for the help of Dua Her and Ramel Hill for their insights into creating a Kickstarter campaign.

To the 131 backers who made this book a reality, thank you from the bottom of my heart.

Support the artist by visiting his online store at

www.touher.com

Also follow him on Instagram @studiotou

and Facebook @studio2estore